'Mike Jones' *Better An Empty House* is a must read for anyone thinking of investing in property. There are plenty of people out there that will sell you courses to "get rich quick" out of property, but in my experience, many of them have gone bust as they haven't understood the basics.

It's not an "armchair investment", there is no get rich quick scheme that works ongoing. It requires building a good team of experts around you—like Mike—so you can avoid the pitfalls so many so-called "property gurus" and investors have fallen foul of. This book gives great practical advice, is easy to digest and most importantly has some cracking case studies to learn from.'

Kate Faulkner—Managing Director, Propertychecklists.co.uk

'I found *Better An Empty House* a really good read. Pitched just right and something I wish had been around when we first started all those years ago. Everything is well-explained in layman's terms and designed to enlighten in a methodical comprehensive manner. Plenty of information, not too much to bamboozle, but enough to encourage potential landlords to appreciate the legality of their role, the importance of the right choice of property and advantage of a good agent.

The book illustrates that being a successful landlord, in any guise, is not for the faint hearted and is certainly not necessarily a way to make a quick buck. Often in with one hand and out with the other but hopefully overall providing a decent return on a long-term investment.'

DL—Hampshire landlord

Better an Empty House Than An Unruly Tenant
A Guide for Landlords
Mike Jones

ISBN 978-1-914603-23-5 (Paperback)
ISBN 978-1-914603-24-2 (EPUB ebook)
ISBN 978-1-914603-25-9 (PDF ebook)

Cover design © 2022 Waterside Press. Created by Christine Hammacott: book-design.co.uk

Main UK distributor Gardners Books, 1 Whittle Drive, Eastbourne, BN23 6QH. Tel: (+44) 01323 521777; sales@gardners.com; www.gardners.com

North American distribution Ingram Book Company, One Ingram Blvd, La Vergne, TN 37086, USA. Tel: (+1) 615 793 5000; inquiry@ingramcontent.com

Cataloguing In-Publication Data A catalogue record for this book can be obtained from the British Library.

Printed by Severn, Gloucester, UK.

Ebook *Better An Empty House Than An Unruly Tenant* is available as an ebook including through library models.

Published 2022 by
Waterside Press Ltd
Sherfield Gables
Sherfield on Loddon, Hook
Hampshire RG27 0JG.

Telephone +44(0)1256 882250
Online catalogue WatersidePress.co.uk
Email enquiries@watersidepress.co.uk

Better an empty house than an unruly tenant

A GUIDE FOR LANDLORDS

Mike Jones

Foreword Dorian Gonsalves

≈ WATERSIDE PRESS

Contents

Publisher's note   *x*

Acknowledgements   *xi*

About the author   *xiii*

About the author of the Foreword   *xiv*

Foreword   *xv*

Preface   *xvii*

Dedication   *xix*

1   **What Type of Landlord Are You?**..21

Type 1: The 'Accidental Landlord'   *21*

Type 2: The 'Lucky Landlord'   *25*

Type 3: The Property Investor   *27*

Conclusion   *29*

2   **The Name(s) on the Deeds** 31

Joint Tenants Versus Tenants in Common   *32*

3   **Risks Associated with Letting Property**....................................33

You Aren't Making a Profit   *33*

No Demand for the Property   *34*

Voids   *36*

Rent Default   *36*

Tenants Abusing the Property   *37*

Fair Wear and Tear   *37*

Flood and Fire   *38*

Tenants Not Vacating   *38*

Distress For Rent Act   *39*

Legislation   *39*

'Cannabis Farms'   *40*

Putting Risks Into Perspective   *40*

Conclusion   *41*

4   **How to Establish Your Budget**...43

Existing Home Loan   *43*

Interest-only Mortgages   *44*

Buy-to-let Mortgages   *44*

Mortgage Criteria   *45*

Interest   *45*

Leveraging   *47*

So to Your Budget — How Much?   *50*

5   **Tenure**...53

Freehold   *53*

Leasehold   *54*

Shared Ownership   *60*

What Tenure is Best for Investment Purposes?   *60*

The Grenfell Effect   *61*

My Flat in Andover   *62*

Conclusion   *63*

6   **Sourcing Your Property**...65

Sales Agent   *65*

Below Market Value   *67*

Auctions   *69*

Short Leases   *70*

7   **Yield**...71

8   **Rental Expectations**..73

9   **Tenant Profiles**..75

1. First-timers   *76*

2. Week-dayers   *78*

3. Long-termers   *79*

4. Students *80*

5. Sharers *80*

6. Secondees from overseas *81*

7. 'The Happy Tenant' *82*

8. 'Mr Blue-Chip' *83*

9. 'The Tenant from Hell' *84*

Restrictions *85*

Referencing *87*

Finding a Tenant *87*

Discrimination *88*

10 **How Big?**..89

Annexes and Studios *89*

One-bed Apartments/Houses/Maisonettes *90*

Two-bed Apartments/Houses *91*

Three-bed Houses *92*

Four-bed (Plus) Houses *93*

Changing Properties in Order to Let *94*

11 **More on Property Types: Merits and Demerits**....................95

More About Annexes *95*

Studios/Flats/Maisonettes/Apartments *96*

Upstairs or Downstairs? *97*

Terraced or Semi-detached? *97*

Detached Properties *99*

Character Properties *99*

12 **Location**...101

Local Facilities *101*

Population *102*

Schools *102*

Risk of Flooding *103*

Shops, Pubs and Entertainment *103*

Trains, Buses and Taxis *104*

Parking *105*

Access to the National Road Network *106*

Conclusion   *106*

13 **The Property Itself**.. 107

Furnished or Unfurnished? *108*

Décor *110*

Floor Covering *112*

Bathrooms *116*

Kitchens *122*

Washing Machines *126*

Additional Sockets *126*

Lighting *127*

Curtains and Blinds *128*

Television *129*

Heating and Drying *130*

Carbon Monoxide and Smoke Detectors *132*

Windows *133*

The Garden *133*

Driveway and Garages *136*

Loft Spaces *137*

Repairing Obligations *138*

Are You Compromising Any of the Issues in
    Chapter 13? *139*

14 **Condensation Mould** 141

What is Condensation? *141*

Lifestyle Adjustments *142*

Back to That 1960s House … *144*

My Landlord's Flat *145*

Another Example: This Time Tenant-related *148*

Conclusion *148*

15   **Preparing Your Property for Letting**.......................... 149

16   **Inventory, Tenancy Checks and Visits**........................155
     The Inventory   *155*
     Check-in   *158*
     Periodic Visits   *159*
     Check-out   *162*

17   **Insurance** 165
     The Building and Its Contents   *165*
     Liability   *165*
     Rent Default Insurance   *166*

18   **Tenancy Agreements** 169
     Lodging Agreement/Licence   *169*
     Assured Shorthold Tenancy   *170*
     Contractual Tenancy   *172*
     Updating Agreements   *173*
     Renewals   *173*
     Always Take Advice   *175*

19   **Sub-letting: Another Cautionary Note**.................... 177
     My Experience of Sub-letting   *178*

20   **Marketing**... 179
     The Folly of Dual Marketing   *180*
     Asking Too Much   *181*
     Another Real Life Case   *182*
     Guaranteed Rent   *182*

21   **Deposits** 183
     How to Deal With a Deposit   *183*
     Deposit Schemes   *184*
     What is the Deposit For?   *184*
     An Example of Landlord Who Was 'Caught Out'   *185*

How Much Should the Deposit Be?   *185*

Lifetime Deposits   *187*

Deposit Deduction Disputes   *187*

My Show Home Landlord   *188*

The Lottery that is Arbitration   *189*

An Extreme Example of Woe   *190*

22   **The Law of Landlord and Tenant**.. 193

Homes (Fitness for Human Habitation) Act 2018   *194*

A Common Often Overlooked Example   *195*

GDPR and the Information Commissioner   *197*

Registration of Landlords   *197*

Retaliatory Eviction and the Deregulation Act 2015   *197*

Right to Rent   *198*

Gas Safety (Installation and Use) Regulations
1996/1998   *199*

Electrical Equipment Regulations   *199*

Fire Safety of Furniture and Furnishings   *200*

Legionella   *200*

Non-Resident Tax   *201*

Minimum Energy Efficiency Standard (MEES)   *202*

The Government White Paper   *203*

23   **Expert Advice**...205

Selecting an Agent   *206*

Questions to Ask Agents   *210*

To Bear in Mind If Thinking of 'Going it Alone'   *214*

Epilogue   *215*

Index   *217*

Publisher's note

The views contained in this book are those of the author and not necessarily shared by the publisher. As stated throughout the book, readers should always take independent advice before embarking on property ventures. Small variations in circumstances may have considerable implications. Neither the author nor publisher can accept any responsibility if this advice goes unheeded.

Acknowledgements

Running the business has always been a joint effort with my business partner, Andrew Lowery. Without him, I doubt I'd have become a lettings agent. Once it was suggested that I write a book, were it not for Andrew's understanding, I'd never have been able to devote so much time to completing it.

Thanks to the individuals who saw it at various stages and encouraged me to persevere: my wife Laura, my sister Lynne, my buddy Karan, Andrew Lowery who I have already mentioned, a landlord named Bob Pike, one of our team, Carole Archer and Kate Shore (who read it while she was supposed to be working!). And thanks to Sammy Bateman, the publication of whose own book made me determined to finish something I'd started years before she'd ever put pen to paper!

Thanks also to Bryan Gibson and the team at Waterside Press for agreeing to take this on and to right all my various wrongs. And I mustn't forget the ever-patient Christine Hammacott at The Art of Communication for unknowingly causing some of my inspiration and then coming up with the design for the cover. Oh, and 'Coxy', who lent me Bob Mortimer's autobiography to read.

Mike Jones
August 2022

Mike Jones

About the author

Mike Jones' first encounter as a landlord was in 1992 and he has been one continuously for over 20 years. Having experienced the services of letting agents across the UK and believing he could offer a better solution, in 2009 he founded his own agency with a business partner. They are now responsible for a significant portfolio, employ a team of nine, and also run a thriving property sales division.

Having been directly involved in the selection and purchase of hundreds of properties for his clients, Mike Jones has also assisted them by advising on and supervising refurbishments. In *Better An Empty House Than An Unruly Tenant*, he candidly describes his early experiences as an enthusiastic but naïve investor. He also tells readers about his own real-life cases as well as recounting the experiences, both successful and tragic, of other property investors with whom he has had dealings.

The author has been hands-on in every single aspect of the lettings cycle and there is barely an area of this industry where he does not have experience and expertise. He lives in Hampshire where he has worked for the last 20 years.

About the author of the Foreword

Dorian Gonsalves entire career has been devoted to the property industry, having worked his way up through the ranks from a negotiator with a well-known chain of estate agents, progressing into various senior management roles. He also 'clocked-up' a five-year stint as a director of the Property Ombudsman, and in his current position works as Chief Executive Officer of one of the UK's largest, most successful property businesses, which manages over 70,000 rental properties.

Foreword

I have known Mike Jones for over a decade and have always been incredibly impressed by his extensive knowledge of the buy-to-let industry. Mike has a reputation for being straight talking, honest and incredibly knowledgeable and he is well-respected by his peers within the industry. Over the years, he has always gone out of his way to ensure that he has kept up-to-date with the fast-changing regulations that impact landlords and investors and has generously shared his knowledge with clients to help maximise the potential of their investments, as well as providing a consistently high-quality service to tenants.

Working with his business partner, Mike has developed a property management and estate agency business that is now a market leader in his local area, as well as the winner of multiple national industry awards. In my opinion, he is perfectly positioned to write this fantastic new book, which not only shares tips, advice and information about all aspects of the rental industry, but also warns of the challenges, pitfalls and costly errors that can easily arise if landlords and investors make uninformed decisions. Such errors can result in poor property investments as well as hefty fines due to lack of legal compliance. Knowledge is key to success!

Mike Jones' business consistently ranks number one within a network of over 170 offices, which is testimony to his knowledge, skills, determination, and ambition. I was therefore honoured and delighted when he invited me to write a Foreword for this book, which I consider to be very well-written and highly informative. In researching and writing it, he has left no stone unturned, and I am confident that this honest and comprehensive guide will be incredibly useful for anyone who has an interest in property.

Dorian Gonsalves
Spring 2022

Better an Empty House than An Unruly Tenant

Preface

I have met hundreds of landlords and I'm aware that many successful ones are women. I am also acutely aware that lots of tenants and contractors are women. In writing this book, for the sake of ease, I refer to all landlords, tenants, contractors, and the like in the masculine. I hope that you will forgive me this small sin. In the same way, when I refer to a landlord, I mean both or all of them when acting jointly.

What the Book is About

I wrote *Better An Empty House* specifically for those considering investment in a rental property (including buy-to-let) or renting out their existing home (or spare accommodation). Whilst it is the inexperienced who I have most in mind, I hope the book will be of interest to those who have already taken their first tentative steps (and perhaps even to seasoned landlords as a 'refresher'). Much of the content is touched on in almost every conversation I have with potential landlords. Reading it will, I hope, make conversations you have with an agent more rewarding, since you should not need to spend so much time on many of the details I cover.

So, You're Considering Investing in Property

Maybe you've seen TV programmes which make this type of investment look easy. Perhaps you have friends or relatives who are landlords. Or you've seen adverts on social media from property gurus willing to share with you their 'secrets to success'. Whatever your motivation, you'll probably need to know more. I'm *not* going to tempt you with get-rich-quick schemes and I'm not going to make it sound any easier than it is. If that's your aim, there are other sources advertised almost daily on social media and I wish you luck in your endeavours. What I *am* going to do is point you in the right direction and throw some light on the bumps you might expect along the way.

Within the various chapters you'll also find some in-depth, real-life examples of *what not to do*. If I haven't made the mistake myself—and I've made many over the years—then I've probably spoken with an investor who has. I hope that after reading the book you will save time, money and maybe some heartache. You aren't obliged to do as I suggest, but I will go to some lengths to highlight when it might be best not to do as I did, or saw others do.

A Word of Caution

Please bear in mind the ever-changing legislative landscape described in *Chapter 22*, as a consequence of which, rather than providing a definitive position for all eternity, I outline everything in the book as of today and draw your attention to the need for further research into any given field at the time you decide to invest. Even as the book was about to go to press plans for significant change were in the air concerning (among other things) a landlord's right to give notice to leave premises to his tenant. I've also included a number of warnings such as those in *Chapter 3* which looks at Risks Associated With Letting Property. Nonetheless, everything I write about is grounded in personal experience, especially the practical advice I offer across the book, such as severing emotional ties and respecting tenants in *Chapter 1,* budgeting in *Chapter 4,* customer loyalty in *Chapter 13,* and how to prepare your property for letting in *Chapter 15.* This will always be relevant and I hope that you take something away from it.

Mike Jones
August 2022

To the author of the Irish proverb used as the title. I was struggling to find something apt until I read Bob Mortimer's autobiography where he mentions it.

And to all those wishing to get involved in the letting of property. Just don't do as I did!

'Better an empty house than an unruly tenant'—Irish proverb

This seems to be the true origin of the phrase which can also be traced to New Zealand where, as in Ireland, it became a well-known euphemism. In his autobiography, *And Away...* the comedian Bob Mortimer attributed it to his doctor, who perhaps learned it from one of these sources.

CHAPTER 1

What Type of Landlord Are You?

Whilst there is no such thing as a 'typical' or 'average' landlord and no two sets of circumstances are identical. In this book I have divided them into three categories:

- the *accidental landlord;*
- the *lucky landlord;* and
- the *property investor.*

It's important to understand which category you fall into and consider whether my conclusions regarding your circumstances are accurate.

Type 1: The 'Accidental Landlord'

If you currently live in a property and wish to rent it out on a temporary basis, but intend to return to live there later, you are likely to experience a few sleepless nights. You've possibly spent considerable time, effort and money in getting your home exactly as you want it to be and now you are going to let it to someone you don't know and possibly won't even meet. In the lettings industry, you are often referred to as an 'accidental' (or sometimes 'reluctant') landlord. This isn't a derogatory term so much as a pretty accurate assessment of your state of mind. Truth be known, you might not actually want to rent out your property, this course being simply the lesser of two evils (it might otherwise stand empty and deteriorate).

High on your list of concerns will be whether your home will be looked after. A tenant is more likely to take care of a well-presented and obviously well-loved property than somewhere that has had a succession of tenants over a prolonged period and is owned by a landlord who is seemingly unconcerned about the state of it. It is easy to imagine how a tenant will eventually decide that if the landlord doesn't put himself out for basic maintenance and décor, then he probably won't mind if there are a few more marks on the walls, or the carpet isn't quite as clean as it was when that tenant moved in.

Finding a tenant for a property in fabulous order is relatively easy, since a quality applicant will probably not consider a sub-standard home. You have, in effect, set out your stall with a quality offering and a price to match, so you'll be likely to attract like-minded individuals; those appreciative of your efforts and prepared to take good care of your property. Nonetheless, there is no guarantee that, when you return, it will be just as you left it. Assume that there will be some decorative works needed at the end of the tenancy and that your garden will no longer be up to Chelsea Flower Show standards. If you leave a property furnished, you'll undoubtedly, especially after a lengthy period, have lost knives and forks, gained a can-opener or two, found an entirely different toaster on the worktop and will be unable to entertain friends using matching tumblers. The income you receive in rent, however, should go a considerable way towards lessening the blow. But, more importantly, you haven't had to sell the property, which may have been the alternative.

Not all accidental landlords have a home ideally suited to the letting market. They are possibly someone for whom creating the ideal letting proposition, attractive to tenants, may prove difficult. There is invariably less enthusiasm for the expense associated with changing a bathroom, a kitchen, carpets, or carrying out re-decoration works on a property in which a landlord has lived and when the perception is that the only person to benefit from such changes is the tenant. Whilst superficially at least this is understandable, offering a tired or otherwise inappropriate property will invariably result in more difficulty in your search for suitable tenants as well as a lower than anticipated rent.

The precise lengths to which you are prepared to go to make your home as attractive as possible to tenants will depend upon your own circumstances. Associated costs are a major contributory factor as indeed is the period for which you expect to be renting out your home. Someone going to work abroad for six months will be far less enthusiastic about fitting a new bathroom, whereas someone relocating for six years is quite likely to consider spending, say, £1,000 on new carpets.

When you *sell* a property, the new owner may well change the bathroom, kitchen, the floor-coverings, and décor. No doubt any offer to buy it will have taken this into consideration. The buyer will have chosen your home because he can see potential or loves the layout. Your personal taste isn't necessarily that important. When you *rent out* your home, however, a tenant cannot change an avocado bathroom suite or that fussy flowery wallpaper. He must live with it and so won't be willing to pay quite as much as if the entire property were to his liking. Depending upon the work you have chosen *not to do,* a good number of prospective tenants will simply continue to look elsewhere. Always remember, you are not marketing your home in isolation. There will be other, similarly priced, properties from which a tenant may choose. And no matter your perceived valuation, it's worth precisely what someone is prepared to pay in rent.

My experience as an accidental landlord

I first dipped my toes into the lettings marketplace as an accidental landlord in 1992 when my wife and I had decided to live and work in Saudi Arabia. In all fairness, we hadn't spent thousands of pounds on creating a fabulous home. We'd bought at the height of a boom in 1988 and simply affording the mortgage (which at one stage hit the dizzying heights of 15% interest) prevented us from even considering spending more on improvements. Whilst we loved our home, we weren't houseproud. We didn't insist that guests removed their shoes when they visited us. We used to hold lively parties and barbecues and, being a smoker myself at the time, we even allowed smoking indoors.

We carried out absolutely no research when we made the decision to let it out. We simply called in a local independent letting agent whose boards we'd seen and allowed them deal with it all. Since we were going to return (at an as yet undetermined time) in the future, we let the property fully-furnished. We removed only those items which were obviously personal and took away high value items such as the stereo system, leaving everything else. Our main driver behind this decision was one of cost; storing everything away for what turned out to be nearly six years would have been expensive and inconvenient.

We received no advice regarding preparation of the property (*Chapter 15*) although to present it in the best light we decorated throughout. I distinctly remember the day our inventory was prepared (*Chapter 16*). The lovely lady who ran the agency came around and 'made a note' of everything which was being left. No photographs were taken, and it comprised no more than four or five pages of brief descriptions which were simply stapled to the back of the tenancy agreement. We must have been ideal landlords in that we allowed the agent to simply get on with whatever was required, and we questioned nothing. Today I have several landlords like this, and they are absolutely the best. No question!

For some long-forgotten reason, we met our first tenants the day they moved in. It was a sunny afternoon, and my wife and I were standing in the back garden with the agent chatting about nothing in particular when the tenants' five-year-old child appeared from the garage with a spade and proceeded to dig a hole in the lawn. Such an introduction to the concept of a tenant not looking after a property wasn't ideal, but we had already accepted that we would need to do some work on our home when we returned. Considering we'd been so lackadaisical in our approach to everything, we did well. Despite several changes of tenant we had no periods without rent coming in with which to contend ('voids': see *Chapter 3*), and when we eventually moved back into the property it was actually in better condition than it would have been if we'd continued living there ourselves. So far as I'm aware, every tenant had the deposit returned in full. But in all honesty, I genuinely don't know since we took no interest in the process at all.

I can now see that we were unbelievably naïve. That we came through the experience unscathed was down to sheer luck. We were fortunate enough to have chosen, at random, an agent who was able to secure a series of good tenants. Those tenants paid their rent on time each and every month and, it would seem, never had lively parties or barbecues. And at least one of them knew sufficient about gardening to repair minor damage to areas laid to lawn. Our story, however, could have had a less successful outcome. It is right to try and be as relaxed about things as you can, but don't be tempted to be quite as cavalier in approach to letting out your most valuable asset.

Even if we'd had the inclination, in 1992 landlords weren't easily able to check out agents as they are nowadays. We certainly didn't have Google on our telephones! The rental market existed, but it wasn't as large. There might have been less able and even unscrupulous agents, but the majority were small businesses, and with far less regulation to worry about, more time on their hands to run efficient agencies and put largely nice and sensible tenants together with reasonable property owners. Today's landscape is different and most available properties are warm, safe and comfortable. The modern-day lettings landscape is about as far removed from that of 1992 as it is possible to be, and it is only going to become more competitive, more complicated, more regulated, and riskier.

This doesn't mean that you shouldn't rent out your property temporarily. Just be sure you can square doing this with the idea that a series of complete strangers will be living in your home and possibly surrounded by your belongings. And accept that you might not be quite as fortunate as we were.

Type 2: The 'Lucky Landlord'

I refer to the landlord who is moving away permanently as a 'lucky' landlord since he is in the fortunate position of being able to fund a second mortgage (or perhaps doesn't need one) with the help of the rent from his first property. If you currently live in a property you wish to let out and to which you intend never to return, then from the minute you decide to go ahead start treating your home as a bricks and mortar investment. It is simply a business. Rather like the owner-occupier who will one day return, you might have spent effort and money getting your home just so. But in your circumstances it is easier to treat this as an attractive feature, which should attract a better tenant and a higher rent. You really must sever all emotional ties as soon as possible. Your property is going to feel progressively less like your home. By all means arrange to make periodic visits — indeed, these are a must for a hundred and one reasons (*Chapter 16*) — but making sure that it is just the same as it used to be is not one of them. Treating your property dispassionately will save you an awful lot of future heartache.

I can think of one example where a tenant improved a property at his own expense by replacing some carpets. Unfortunately, he hadn't sought the landlord's consent and the latter was livid, since they were no longer those his mother had installed 20 years ago! Most landlords would have been pleasantly shocked but have understanding of the tenant's desire to live in a home with presentable carpets. Apart from anything else, it's indicative that a tenant wishes to stay long-term and what sort of landlord doesn't want long-term tenants? Neither the landlord nor his mother would ever set foot in the property again. He really should have been able to take a step back and see the improvement for what it was.

At an appointment to appraise such a property, I always ask a landlord whether he has any intention of returning to live in it *one day*. This is so that I can establish his motivations and possible concerns, and to gently help re-frame his mind-set. Every now and then I speak with a landlord who wants to let his property because he is about to set up home with his partner and, whilst he doesn't necessarily think he'll ever come back, there seems to be that nagging doubt in his mind. If this is you, then try and accept that the break-up of a relationship will be disruptive and whilst it may be unhelpful to come back to a property that is no longer 'just-so', you still have a property to which you can beat your retreat. Keeping it just as you liked it on the off chance that you'll one day return isn't terribly helpful in investment terms. And it might not be the right frame of mind to have when setting-up house with a new partner! But that's a subject for another book.

My experience as a 'lucky' landlord

In 2005, my wife and I were 'lucky'. We were running a business based in Dorchester and had decided to return to the Winchester area 50 miles away. We were living in what was only ever intended to be a temporary home; a two-bed apartment in a converted Victorian hospital. I wasn't yet a letting agent, but my then business was going well, and we were fortunate enough to be in the position of affording a higher than necessary mortgage on the new house whilst still keeping the apartment. Drawing on the 'vast' experience of the previous time we let a property, we went about things in almost the same cavalier manner. And why wouldn't we when it had been so easy first time around? The only real difference was the way in which we selected an agent. This time we knew someone from the local pub who worked for an agent in Dorchester.

We'd only owned the apartment since 2002 and had no emotional attachment to it, so we had no fears regarding its treatment and the day we moved out it became an investment. For some reason best known to ourselves we'd painted our bathroom in a hideous dark blue. Shortly after the first tenancy began, we had a request to re-decorate it. It never crossed our minds to be concerned that someone was altering our apartment. Someone with better sense wanted to 'sort it out' and we merrily agreed. By the same token, had they wished to change the magnolia in the living room we'd have been equally content.

I will be referring over and again in this book to the 'happy tenant' who I say more about in *Chapter 9*. My mantra is that a happy tenant is a good tenant. He pays his rent, on time, generally looks after the place and stays longer. If blue or magnolia doesn't make him happy, then let him change it. An unhappy tenant who is forced to put up with a hideous bathroom might easily start to find fault with other things and a landlord who doesn't oblige might well find himself in receipt of regular complaints about 'faults'. What I call a tenant's 'wish-list'.

Type 3: The Property Investor

You're buying a property specifically as an investment, or you already have out-and-out investment properties. Here your approach ought to be easier than that of a former owner-occupier who may still be attached to what was his 'own home'.

The 'part-time' investor

Probably the most common type of property investor is someone who has a full-time job, pension or other private income, and as a side line is, say, using a windfall of some description to enable him to buy somewhere to let. Maybe there is a lump sum from his pension, redundancy pay or an inheritance, or he may have downsized his own residence and have spare funds, and/or possibly he has decided to take out a buy-to-let mortgage (*Chapter 4*). He may have one or more properties. But no matter how many he continues to regard it as supplementary to his day-to-day business, job or lifestyle.

His approach is subtly different to that of the full-time investor (below). He is possibly quite experienced in that he may have several properties and has been letting out for some while, but he is still likely to be reliant upon an agent to conduct the day-to-day management of his tenancies.[1] He is probably conservative in his approach to investing and, whilst he might eventually use equity to raise further deposits to purchase additional properties, he is unlikely to employ some of the more aggressive approaches used by a full-time investor. Repairs, renewals, renovation works, and minor alterations are considered solely upon their financial merits and the needs of the tenant or property. Emotional attachment is generally entirely absent.

The 'full-time' investor

No matter how this investor started out, at some stage he decided to move up a gear or two and now no longer relies upon a job outside of his property empire. His portfolio is of such a magnitude that it can support him financially. Fergus and Judith Wilson of Ashford in Kent are two famous investors fitting into this category. Former teachers, they built an enormous portfolio in that county, on occasions apparently buying almost entire developments of new homes. They reportedly sold their portfolio of 900 homes for £250 million.

Full-time investors may employ 'aggressive' strategies, searching for below market value properties to buy. This frequently allows for the fast release of the original deposit to fund another purchase. Sometimes, quite extreme 'leveraging' (*Chapter 4*) is employed. As you will read later, this is useful in a rising market and can have dramatic effects on the value of a portfolio. It can, however, lead to catastrophic downfalls in a falling market. As I said in the Preface, letting isn't generally about getting rich quickly. I haven't yet explained how the leveraging I mention works, but it's common for the more sophisticated methods to be sold to individuals equipped neither financially, emotionally nor intellectually. Even the outwardly most successful of investors can get investments spectacularly wrong.

I also built a portfolio

Having been both an accidental landlord and a lucky landlord, I embarked on a plan to create a property portfolio of my own. I might originally have harboured dreams of total independence, but I fell into the category of continuing

---

1. Throughout this book and in the case of leasehold property, routine *day-to-day management tasks* by the property owner or his agent, such as repairs or replacements under the tenancy agreement, must be contrasted with the *management of the freehold, its structure and associated obligations* by the freeholder, his agent or management company: see *Chapter 5*, Tenure.

to have a proper job to support my lifestyle and now treat my portfolio as a supplement to my pension provisions.

Buying inappropriately without seeking proper advice became my hallmark and is the reason my own portfolio is nowhere near as successful as it might have been had I conducted proper research. Many of the landlords with whom I deal each day have been guilty of this approach to a greater or lesser degree. Like myself, however, they are often too far down a particular road to do much about it. It's difficult to change tack when someone who is retired has an interest-only mortgage on an originally over-priced leasehold property where his borrowing against it now exceeds its current equity value.

Conclusion

If you proceed, you are or will become one of the above types of landlord. I know landlords who fit exactly into each category, the good, the bad and the ugly among their number. The ones who are doing well, both financially and in terms of their sanity, are those who have embraced their position and accepted that their investment is simply bricks and mortar. They treat the enterprise as a business and have realistic expectations in every regard. They also treat their tenants with respect and are responsible and reasonable in their approach to the entire subject.

CHAPTER 2

The Name(s) on the Deeds

A major consideration when contemplating a property purchase is how you own it, especially if more than one person or entity is involved. This is a subject on which you should quite definitely take professional advice from an accountant and solicitor before agreeing to anything. Related to how the property is owned (or 'held' in legal parlance) there can also be various implications regarding capital gains tax (CGT), inheritance tax (IHT)/succession, and personal taxation on lettings income. Depending on its value when purchased you also need to be aware of Stamp Duty Land Tax (Stamp Duty) which is payable by the buyer at the outset above a prescribed level.[1] All this in addition to legal, conveyancing Land Registry and local authority search fees. A separate yet connected issue is 'tenure'—whether freehold or leasehold (*Chapter 5*).

For example, you can own a property as an individual, through a partnership, a limited company or sometimes a pension scheme or trust. I often suggest Google as the source of further information, but on this occasion if you don't understand the various implications, I would urge caution and suggest that you use the internet only to point you in the right direction and not for a definitive answer. There is much misinformation in the 'ether' and there can be significant financial implications if you go about things in the wrong way. Taxation, especially, is something which has a habit of changing periodically. I hope that what follows is helpful.

---

1. For the current stamp duty threshold and tax tables, see: www.gov.uk/stamp-duty-land-tax/residential-property-rates; for CGT on property that is not your main home: https://www.gov.uk/tax-sell-property; and for IHT see www.gov.uk/inheritance-tax

Joint Tenants Versus Tenants in Common

A legal issue which is often overlooked, but which is simple to address is the question of whether a property should be owned as 'joint tenants' or 'tenants in common'. If you are married or in a stable long-term relationship and you elect to purchase as joint tenants, then upon the death of one party the right of survivorship applies, and the property is automatically inherited by the survivor. In the case of business partners, or where perhaps it is a relatively new relationship, you should give serious thought to owning as tenants in common as described below. Additionally, if one or more of the purchasers was married before, then you might also like to consider a tenancy in common which clearly separates out your share.

Simply put, as tenants in common, you can own the property in differing percentages. So, if it is a business arrangement and one party puts in 25% of the deposit and the other contributes 75%, you might decide to own the property in a ratio of 25% to 75%. Upon your own death, you might wish to leave your share of the property to children say from a previous marriage, or in the case of a business relationship to your wife or civil partner. Owning a property as tenants in common allows you to make these choices. Even if neither party dies, they may still wish to part company at some stage and owning as joint tenants may well end up needing the involvement of the courts, since one party may wish to keep the property whilst the other wishes to sell. Where circumstances change and one party becomes more involved financially than the other, as tenants in common you can adjust the percentage split in ownership.

Sometimes a solicitor will advise or allow a purchase to go ahead as joint tenants, since it can be easier. It is possible to change arrangements after the event but moving from one form of tenure to the other can be more difficult than if done correctly at the outset. So, if you do want to own in a particular way, make this clear to your conveyancer and be sure to study his advice concerning your exact situation.

CHAPTER 3

Risks Associated with Letting Property

Before I go any further, I'll 'head off at the pass' those of you who think that, even if it's not a get-rich scheme, letting is relatively easy and little can go wrong. No matter how well-prepared you or your property are, how much advice you take and how careful you are, letting-out properties is not without risk. Some of the risk may be mitigated by a prudent approach, but sometimes a negative outcome is simply down bad luck. Events may conspire in our favour but sometimes they conspire against us. It really can be as simple as that.

In the same way that TV is often a catalyst for property investment, it can also provide examples of where things went horribly wrong as demonstrated by Paul Shamplina in his online presentations.[1] So, what are some of the risks?

You Aren't Making a Profit

Landlords don't usually discuss the intricacies of their personal finances with me, but I suspect that a fair proportion have arranged matters such that there is little, or no, contingency built into their budget. I read almost daily on internet forums about novices being advised by others and, quite frankly, it often discloses incredibly bad advice. If something seems 'too good to be true', it inevitably is. Property investment is no exception.

Property should almost invariably be a long-term investment and good sound financial planning is paramount. Unless you have a sizeable deposit and funds in reserve to cover the unexpected then, as a beginner, you should really give

---

1. See: www.landlordaction.co.uk

serious thought to whether this is an appropriate investment *for you*. On one or two occasions I have actually said to investors that they would be better off putting their money into Premium Bonds. If the sums of money you are considering investing in property don't comfortably cover the cost of you and your partner buying the maximum number of Premium Bonds[2] then I strongly suggest that you stick to National Savings & Investments.

Decisions that are made on a shoestring are rarely well thought out. Budget for less income and expect higher expenses. Leave a healthy margin. Always. Fly by the seat of your pants at your peril. You'll either have barely sufficient wriggle-room to get through the lettings exercise, or you'll end up with what might easily grow into insurmountable financial difficulties.

It's perhaps tempting to somehow pass the pain on to your tenant. This might be directly through increased rents or indirectly through less frequent refurbishments or delays in responding to maintenance issues. By the time you've finished this book, I hope you'll understand my views on such a stance. But, for the moment, let me just suggest that you ought really to avoid getting yourself in such a position in the first place.

Sometimes, a deal doesn't shape up quite as intended and another way of improving your margin is to try and force an agent to act at a reduced fee. Imagine being the agent and having a prospective tenant lined up who is suited to two properties. On one you have a fair margin and on the other you are being expected to subsidise a landlord's error of judgement. Which will be the letting you are most keen to fill? And even were you to find a tenant on reduced margins, would you be likely to go the extra yard for that landlord?

No Demand for the Property

You might well end up taking the best advice, buy the best possible property, prepare it to a good specification, and then find that it comes to the market at precisely the same time as 30 others do: all seemingly identical properties that other people have decided, for whatever reason, to let for £50 a month less than

---

2.   Currently (2022) £50,000 per person: see www.nsandi.com

you were planning to. You'll either be incredibly fortunate or find yourself having to accept a lower rent, or a long wait for suitable tenants.

My then business partner and I invested in two properties in Preston, Lancashire in 2006. They looked like fantastic properties and indeed were finished to a high standard. What, as novices ourselves, we failed to realise was that the developer was releasing some 200 at the same time. Rather than the phased release that had been promised, Preston was suddenly awash with fantastic new, two-bed properties. To add insult to injury, a further two developments came to market at almost the same time. Fortunately, we were able to weather the seven-month storm that ensued as our properties lay empty, gathering dust. But living hundreds of miles away in Hampshire, we were unable to keep popping into the local agents responsible for marketing them, a necessary act in these circumstances.

In Basingstoke in 2019, a similar situation arose. By then I was an agent myself and we were inundated with calls from landlords all of whom believed their apartments to be worth considerably more than they were, and all of which came to market within weeks of each other. There were dozens of unhappy landlords, reluctant to believe what they were being advised and some of their apartments lay empty for months.

Sometimes you can do something constructive to alleviate this. Consider making your property stand out from the crowd by offering an initial rent-free or discounted period. But don't necessarily reduce the rent for the whole of the tenancy because, if your tenant stays, you'll find it harder to get back to market rent, whereas a one-off financial hit won't affect your ability to add a modest increase later to keep pace with the market. In Preston, we continually attempted to reduce the price of our apartments, but none of the agents in town was interested. Try marketing properties yourself at arm's length — it's practically impossible when there is a 'glut'. Apparently, we would have 'lowered the value' of the development. Eventually all their rents were reduced, but bad advice meant that at least two novices paid dearly.

There are countless other reasons why a property may lie empty (known as a 'void': see next section) for extended periods. Hopefully, you will learn from this book about the need to ensure that the property you are considering is appropriate and at least gives you a fighting chance. Size, type, location, the property's presentation and price all play their part in this. I mentioned earlier my theory about events sometimes conspiring against landlords. Assume this will be the case for you. Budget for longer initial periods with no rent coming in and a lower rent than you had anticipated when it does come on stream. Hope for the best but prepare for the worst.

Voids

Void period is the description given in the lettings industry to a stretch of time when no rent is coming in. The financial effects are the same as when there is no demand for a property (above), but other factors come into play. For example, it might be caused by a tenant postponing a tenancy start date. They might wish to push it back by a couple of weeks which might not give you sufficient time to find an alternative tenant. Or, you might have refurbishment works that over-run. Maybe your carpet fitter lets you down or you can't get the replacement boiler installed in time. There can be all manner of reasons why you have no rental income. Even the best property can have occasional voids between tenancies, but there will be periods of unexpected and inexplicable voids. If you have borrowings, or you are reliant upon rental income, pay particular attention to *Chapter 4* on budgeting.

Rent Default

Tenants not paying their rent is another factor that can disrupt a landlord's income. This can occasionally happen even with the best of tenants, none of us is immune to redundancy or illness. Prudent referencing of tenants (*Chapter 20*) will help save you from rogue tenants. Fortunately, it is possible to insure against non-payment of rent (*Chapter 17*).

Covid-19 might be an extreme cause of rent arrears, but it graphically demonstrated just how fragile your average individual's finances are. It is common, apparently, for someone's reserves to amount to only a few weeks' worth of running costs. How would you fare were you to have no income for a month or so? Once again, this illustrates the need for reserves. Even when you *are* covered by insurance, there will inevitably be cashflow issues whilst the insurance process is dealt with (and please be aware that many insurers won't cover the first month and will charge you an 'excess' when you claim against their policy).

Tenants Abusing the Property

Proper referencing helps eliminate much of this, but once again a determined rogue tenant may slip through the net. And a tenant's personal circumstances may easily alter; events might take a turn and change him into a less than ideal one. Regular visits to monitor the way in which the property is being kept will enable you to spot issues, hopefully before they get out of hand (*Chapter 16*).

Whatever happens, be prepared to 'take it on the chin' and strive to bring your property back up to scratch straightaway. If you don't act immediately, you'll either not find tenants to take the property on at an acceptable rent, or you'll attract sub-standard tenants. Either of these results will end in tears and you'll be forced to address the abuse sooner or later, so deal with it now and save yourself the grief. Dare I mention the need for reserves again?

Fair Wear and Tear

Even if your property doesn't suffer from out-and-out abuse, there will be accidental damage and wear and tear. And, if you read *Chapter 21* on deposits, you'll discover that you might not get the outcome that you would like if it comes to a dispute. Yet it's worth bearing in mind that most tenants are reliable and honest individuals, but the person most likely to look after your property well is you. Therefore, expect wear and tear to be somewhat greater than it would be if you were to live in the premises yourself. Forget how long the decorations in your own home last. You're unlikely to find that staircase walls stay fresh for quite as long when a property is tenanted. There are recognised lengths of time that decorations are supposed to last and these can be important when trying to claim against a tenant's deposit (see again *Chapter 21*).

Flood and Fire

This sort of event does happen occasionally, although it can also occur in an owner-occupied home. It might be argued that a tenant is likely to be less careful than an owner-occupier, but I'm not sure that anyone would volunteer to have belongings damaged by fire or water. Once again, you can insure against these perils.

Tenants Not Vacating

Your tenant may not leave on time when the tenancy expires or want to give you back your property at the end of the tenancy. Nowadays it is relatively straightforward to gain possession of a property when a landlord wishes to return there or sell it. Under the Housing Act 1988 he may use a 'Section 21 notice' to gain possession without the need to provide the tenant with a reason. Sometimes referred to in the press as a 'no-fault' notice, this is likely to be removed from the statute book as I explain in *Chapter 22*. So please note that everything I say here must be viewed in the light of any such changes, if and when they happen. It is my fervent belief that Parliament will create progressively more and more risk to the private landlord over coming years.

In my experience, landlords rarely want to evict tenants without good reason and it is my belief that there will continue to be ways in which they may be able to rid themselves of troublesome ones, no matter what the reason. Housing Act 1988 'Section 8 notices' are currently used when applying to a court for possession because of non-payment of rent, or on other grounds. If this procedure is removed by Parliament (*Chapter 22*), then Section 8 Notices will I believe have to be given added mandatory grounds. For some Section 8 Notices, the courts currently have discretionary powers not to grant possession.

All these notices take time to serve and take effect and it may be that you will still need to apply to courts as the notices in themselves don't give automatic possession. Again, in my experience, most tenants will leave of their own accord at the end of the notice period of a Section 21 notice, but not all do.

Distress For Rent Act

This might not seem like a risk, but it does occasionally happen and can influence the starting date of a following tenancy. There can be knock-on effects and several people inconvenienced. There is, however, a little-known piece of legislation (Section 18 of the Distress for Rent Act 1737) that allows you to charge a tenant double rent under these circumstances. Please take advice, however, since you cannot receive monies after the end date as 'rent' and you cannot do anything which would make the tenant believe that he is still a tenant. You effectively need to treat him as a trespasser. I suggest that you err on the side of caution, be careful in what you say to him and try and establish what his intentions are. It may be that he himself has been let down and that time and regular communication will resolve the situation to the satisfaction of all parties. In some circumstances, the prospect of a landlord relying on this piece of legislation is sufficient to ensure a tenant moves out when required. But, of course, you need to have a pretty good idea that this is a likely situation. You can't simply threaten each and every tenant!

Legislation

There is insufficient space in this book to list and explain the hundreds of pieces of legislation which affect landlords and tenants nowadays. Suffice it to say that a landlord faces unlimited fines, imprisonment, and a banning order where breaches of legislation are significant. Furthermore, there are pieces of legislation nowadays which affect a landlord's ability to serve a Section 21 notice. So, even if a landlord isn't fined or imprisoned, he may find himself unable to get possession and his tenant might have the authority to stay in the landlord's property for as long as he wishes. Legislation is perhaps a far bigger risk than the average landlord appreciates. Even using a lettings agent to manage his tenancy might not insulate him entirely from the threat of penalties. I say more about what lawyers call 'The Law of Landlord and Tenant' in *Chapter 22*.

'Cannabis Farms'

We have all probably seen examples on TV of the situation where someone uses property for growing cannabis. Despite this being a relatively uncommon practice, insufficient due diligence at the referencing stage, a lack of regular visits, and in particular alertness at the first such visit, are likely contributors to their existence. Be careful of anyone volunteering to pay an inflated rent, being not at all concerned about a property's condition or with soaring electricity use. Whatever you do, don't turn a blind-eye.

Putting Risks Into Perspective

Having said that no letting is without risk, I ought to put this into some sort of perspective. What follows is based upon my experience of some 3,200 tenancies. I have come across only one small cannabis farm and this was in a neighbouring property and not one where I had any involvement. If you allow me to ignore an incident where a three-year-old child set fire to the landlord's shed and the neighbour's fence, then in the same period, I have only had two experiences of fires. Although, I also had a situation where a wayward toaster caused some minor heat damage to kitchen cabinets (see *Chapter 13* for advice on avoiding this and what and what not to provide to a tenant).

I do come across water leaking into downstairs apartments occasionally and I did have three apartments rendered uninhabitable by this twice in quick succession, but all were largely covered by insurance policies. In 2021, I also came across a DIY-installed pair of bidet attachments which caused a major leak in a block of new flats. Installed by a qualified doctor, without the landlord's consent, who carried out plumbing installations as 'a hobby'!

As an aside, you will gather from this book that I detest most flats and apartments with a passion. There are so many reasons why they are an awful investment proposition and being leak magnets is one such. And I admit that I speak from personal experience in this regard. If you take only one thing from this book, let it be that apartments are generally the worst type of property investment.

I have personally been to court regarding unpaid rent on only one occasion. Sadly, this was because the landlord selected a tenant against my better judgement and chose not to insure the risk. We also once purchased a portfolio with a couple of rent arrears issues, but these were caused by the previous letting agent accepting tenants without adequate referencing. On a handful of occasions, a landlord hasn't received all the rent that was due, but the largest of these sums was less than £1,000. The others were a matter of a couple of hundred pounds.

In a few properties, damage has been significant but with only one exception the cost to the landlord was only a few hundred pounds. One was the case where I went to court (see *Chapter 16* concerning inventories), and it wouldn't have happened had the landlord not accepted a sub-standard tenant. Occasionally, I've come across a tenant who is unable or unwilling to vacate exactly in line with a landlord's wishes. I've had one bailiff eviction and a handful where the dates haven't tied in as successfully as I would have liked.

A brief Covid-19 addendum

Covid-19 brought its own rent default issues and I've come across a few, but even so, with one notable exception, the tenants have agreements in place to pay the overdue rent when they are able. The notable exception was caused by a landlord adopting an unhelpful and uncaring stance resulting in the tenant leaving one night, with arrears of £1,400.

Conclusion

In economic terms, profit can be defined as 'the return upon risk to the entrepreneur'. So, risk is endemic to investment. I've touched upon how some of risks may be minimised or mitigated already, but I will explain in far more detail elsewhere in this book the approach a sensible investor might take to return a profit without too much financial danger. I referred to Paul Shamplina's videos at the start of this chapter. Whilst these are obviously real life examples, I hope that you will appreciate by now that, if you conduct your affairs sensibly, such extreme examples ought to be rare indeed.

CHAPTER 4

How to Establish Your Budget

Before looking at a budget, it's important to understand a bit about mortgages and also about leveraging.

Existing Home Loan

It may be that you have an existing mortgage on your property that you arranged when you first bought it. If you are an accidental landlord (*Chapter 1*), it is quite likely that you have such a mortgage in place. You've maybe lived at the property for several years and are now going abroad or further afield in the UK on secondment and you're looking to let out your property until you return. This position may be just as true for the 'lucky' landlord reading what I am about to say.

Approach your lender and seek their 'consent to let'. Depending upon circumstances, you will be charged an administration fee of typically £50 to £200. On occasions, depending upon your own personal circumstances, it may be that your lender wishes you to swap to a 'buy-to-let' product, or insists on your rate of interest being increased. If you are in some form of fixed-rate deal, then this might also complicate their response. Nonetheless, I have yet to come across an individual for whom there wasn't a solution and who wasn't able to secure consent one way or another.

If your lender insists on you changing to a buy-to-let product, however, it may well be worth speaking with an independent mortgage advisor. It may be that looking at the whole of the market discloses something more appropriate to your circumstances than your current provider. It is imperative that you have the consent described above. If, for some reason, you are unable to meet your mortgage obligations your lender will seek to gain possession and possibly sell the property 'over your head'. A tenant in occupation without a lender's consent will cause no end of problems and make it difficult for you to secure borrowings in future.

If you are an accidental landlord, you are likely to have a repayment mortgage of some description. This means that over the lifespan of your mortgage, you will be repaying the capital sum borrowed, together with any interest. It may well prove to be beneficial and certainly cheaper to consider changing your arrangements so that you have an interest-only mortgage of some sort.

Interest-only Mortgages

Most investors use an 'interest-only' mortgage. They simply pay down the interest on the mortgage and whatever sum was originally borrowed is still outstanding at the end of the term. Consequently, an interest-only mortgage is considerably cheaper. This is an important factor to bear in mind, especially if your anticipated rent doesn't adequately cover your mortgage repayments. Changing to interest-only may well enable you to cover your mortgage and have some leeway each month for repairs, renewals, and void periods.

Buy-to-let Mortgages

These are sold specifically for investors or for homeowners whose situations change. They are usually interest-only, although depending upon the terms, you may well be able to repay additional sums and so reduce the capital sum owed. Your mortgage advisor will be able to help you in choosing of a product suited to your own circumstances.

Mortgage Criteria

There are certain considerations that need to be borne in mind, no matter what type of mortgage you secure. A lender will have maximum loan-to-value (LTV) criteria. It may be that you are unable to borrow more than 75% of the value for the property. So, for a £250,000 investment, you will need a deposit of £62,500. The LTV may vary slightly from lender to lender. The lender will also insist that the gross rent covers the mortgage by a certain percentage. Typically, this is 25% or 30%. So, if your mortgage repayments are £500 per month, the rent must be perhaps £625 or £650, depending upon the rules for your lender.

Interest

The amount of interest you pay will depend on the type of loan you ('the mortgagee') choose or a lender ('the mortgagor') agrees to let you take out. Critical, if you are choosing which type of mortgage to apply for, will be your assessment of the economy going forwards, your own financial position, attitude to risk, future intentions and competing rates of interest on loans being offered.

Fixed-rate loans

The rate of interest payable is fixed for a set period, making budgeting that much easier. Often, the longer the term the higher the rate of interest. You need to bear in mind the costs associated with arranging new mortgages over time if you opt for shorter terms at lower rates of interest. These costs vary according to market conditions and can easily vary from a few hundred to a couple of thousand pounds.

Tracker loans

With tracker mortgage loans the rate of interest follows the Bank of England or other bank rate. This might be 0.5% above whatever the prevailing rate of interest is. This means that your payments will go up and down with fluctuations in interest rates. There may or may not be a cap on this rate.

Flexible loans

You may sometimes come across the word 'flexible' attached to a mortgage. What this means will depend on the individual product but it may mean that you can opt to switch from one deal to another at certain points in time, or from a fixed-rate loan to a tracker loan or vice-versa. Contrast, however, the situation whereby 'flexible rate' is used as just another name for a tracker loan.

Interest rates

We have all been lulled into something of a false sense of security. Since the crash of 2006–2008, interest rates have been incredibly low. It is perhaps worth being reminded that historically, and certainly since the 1960s, interest rates have been significantly higher than they are currently. If you are being prudent, you will make your calculations on the basis that in the lifetime of your investment, interest rates are likely to be a fair bit higher than they are now. It's worth noting that loan applications are stress tested to see whether or not the loan would continue to be affordable following a 3% increase in the underlying interest rate (sometimes called the 'base rate'). Figure 1 below shows UK interest rates at 31 December each year from 1979 to 2020.

After an unusual period when there was a zero underlying rate, in February 2022 this rose to 0.5% and by June of that year they stood at 1.25%. The average for the period 1992 to 2004 was 5.5%. How would your investment fare if interest rates were to return to this sort of level? Just how much leeway would it be prudent to allow? This sort of thing depends upon your own attitude to risk. I know of landlords who work based on 6% and I'm not sure that this is such a bad idea. Of course, the capital value of your property (your asset) will, over time, increase. But there are landlords who suffered badly due to the last crash and found their investments worth less than their mortgages.

The Covid-19 pandemic has cost the UK Government billions and, at some stage, these monies will need to be recouped one way or another. Who among us can tell exactly what the longer-term effects will be upon the economy? One thing is for certain, however, and that is that this prolonged period of low interest rates cannot continue ad infinitum. Inflation at the time of writing this book in early-2022 is becoming of concern and the bank base rate is one tool which the Bank of England uses to try and slow down this rise.

Year	%	Year	%	Year	%
1979	17	1993	5.37	2007	5.50
1980	14	1994	6.12	2008	2
1981	14.37	1995	6.37	2009	0.50
1982	10	1996	5.93	2010	0.50
1983	9.06	1997	7.25	2011	0.50
1984	9.50	1998	6.25	2012	0.50
1985	11.37	1999	5.50	2013	0.50
1986	10.87	2000	6	2014	0.50
1987	8.37	2001	4	2015	0.50
1988	12.87	2002	4	2016	0.25
1989	14.87	2003	3.75	2017	0.50
1990	13.87	2004	4.75	2018	0.75
1991	10.37	2005	4.50	2019	0.75
1992	6.87	2006	5	2020	0.10

Figure 1: Bank of England base rate each December 1979 to 2020

Leveraging

I am personally a great advocate of having as small a mortgage as possible. I know several landlords who own properties outright and refuse as a matter of principle to have loans on them. Whilst I accept their stance, I believe that on occasions they miss out on purchases which are slightly out of their reach, but achievable with small loans. I know that there are some who take a more aggressive stance to mortgages and so I am going to explain what is known as 'leveraging'.

For the sake of argument, let's suppose that you can buy a property valued at £100,000 and that you are fortunate enough to be able to pay cash for it. Over a given time, let's suppose that the property increases in value by £10,000. It is now worth £110,000 which is 10% more than you paid for it and your £100,000 cash has therefore given you a 10% return.

	1 Property	2 Properties	
Value now	£110,000	£110,000	£110,000
Purchase price	£100,000	£100,000	£100,000
Cash employed	£100,000	£50,000	£50,000
Increase in value	£10,000	£10,000	£10,000
Return on cash	10%	20%	20%
Mortgage rate (Interest-only)	3%	3%	3%
Annual Rental Income	£6,000	£6,000	£6,000
Annual Mortgage Cost	£0	£1,500	£1,500
Gain from rent	£6,000	£4,500	£4,500
Gain from appreciation	£10,000	£10,000	£10,000
	£16,000	£14,500	£14,500
Total from 2 properties			£29,000
Return on cash employed	16%		29%

Figure 2: Leveraging—The effect when property values increase

Now, let's suppose that an identical property was purchased for £100,000 but using a £50,000 mortgage. The same property increases in value by the same £10,000 to £110,000 and the property is worth the same, i.e. 10% more than it was. But, in this example, the cash that was employed in the deal is less. Only £50,000 in cash was used, which means that the return on the £50,000 is £10,000 or 20%. This is called leveraging.

	1 Property	2 Properties	
Value now	£90,000	£90,000	£90,000
Purchase price	£100,000	£100,000	£100,000
Cash employed	£100,000	£50,000	£50,000
Increase in value	-£10,000	-£10,000	-£10,000
Return on cash	-10%	-20%	-20%
Mortgage rate (Interest-only)	3%	3%	3%
Annual Rental Income	£6,000	£6,000	£6,000
Annual Mortgage Cost	£0	£1,500	£1,500
Gain from rent	£6,000	£4,500	£4,500
Loss from depreciation	-£10,000	-£10,000	-£10,000
	-£4,000	-£5,500	-£5,500
Total from 2 properties			-£11,000
Return on cash employed	-4%		-11%

Figure 3: Leveraging—Showing the risks in a falling market.

For the sake of illustration in both Figure 2 and Figure 3 above, an interest-only mortgage has been assumed at a rate of 3%. And to provide fuller comparison, a rental income of £6,000 per annum. Figure 2 clearly shows that there is a 13% increase in returns by leveraging and buying two properties. In a falling market Figure 3 shows that the loss is 7% greater. So just in case you are thinking that leveraging is always good, not only can it amplify profits in good times, it also magnifies losses when the market turns downwards (and it has a habit of doing this). And, if interest rates were to have risen at the same time, the losses in Figure 3 would have increased further.

Whilst leveraging can enable you to purchase a property that you thought was beyond your financial reach, you should exercise caution and ensure that you do not overstretch yourself. So, please consider whether your budget might need to be re-visited. Remember my tip: be conservative in your income expectations and pessimistic about your expenses (*Chapter 1*). It's far better to be pleasantly surprised when you learn that you're making more than you budgeted for.

So to Your Budget — How Much?

When considering a property purchase, you need to make sure that you include all the likely costs associated with the acquisition, preparation and starting of a tenancy and include some contingency for issues arising before and after the tenancy starts. Don't forget to include the actual mortgage payments as a cost you'll probably need to cover for a while.

- Purchase price
- Survey
- Legal fees
- Stamp Duty Land Tax ('stamp duty')
- Insurance premiums: buildings and contents, landlord's liability, rent default
- Refurbishment works
- Compliance costs: smoke detectors, carbon monoxide detectors
- Energy performance certificate (EPC)
- Gas safety checks

- Electrical safety checks
- Almost inevitable electrical remedial works on older properties
- Legionella risk-assessment
- Inventory preparation
- Agent's fees
- Void periods
- Mortgage arrangement fees
- Mortgage repayments
- Void period utilities
- Void period council tax (after any concessionary period[1])
- Contingencies.

Of course, there may well be other costs to consider. This list is not intended to be exhaustive, but it should help you appreciate the extra expenses you may not have been considering.

I suggest starting a spreadsheet and beginning to put some figures into it. You ought to know how much cash you have, and it might be an idea to speak with a financial advisor to establish the sort of mortgage you'll be able to raise if needed. Remember to be on the conservative side as far as rental income is concerned and get quotes for professional costs, stamp duty, etc. Where you need to estimate costs, ask tradesmen, insurance companies and other suppliers for a sensible idea of likely expenditure. Please don't forget to allow a contingency. This may be as much as 10–15% of your anticipated expenditure. All of this ought to mean you have an idea of the sort of budget you have at your disposal. Don't start with a property price in mind, since you might end up setting your heart on one and having to cut corners in order to afford it.

Once you have a budget, avoid the temptation to look at properties which will cost more, unless you are convinced that you can negotiate on the asking price. Of course, intending to do without a mortgage then considering one to get something slightly more expensive is potentially a great idea. Before you get too far down the road though and certainly before you commit yourself to any expense, speak with an advisor and get an agreement in principle for a loan.

---

1. The local council may allow three months free for empty unfurnished properties, then maybe three months at a reduced rate of 50 per cent. Water companies may also allow a free period.

CHAPTER 5

Tenure

There are different ways in which you can own (or 'hold') what is known as 'real property' (i.e. land, buildings, premises).[1] This is known as 'tenure'. Which tenure is determined by the seller and may be freehold or leasehold.

Freehold

When you purchase a freehold property, you literally buy it lock stock and barrel. If you were to pay cash for the property, then it would be yours entirely and with it would come all the responsibilities associated with outright ownership. If you were to buy it with a mortgage, then until such time as you finish paying off the loan, you would effectively own part of it, with the remainder being owned by the mortgage lender. Your lender will still expect you to undertake responsibility for everything though, as if you owned it outright. You will be expected to keep the property in a good state of repair and to insure it.

Some of your obligations might be shared with your neighbours. For example, you might be responsible for fences to one side of the property and a neighbour would be responsible for the other side, or it might be that you share the cost of fencing. You won't really have dealings with any third party, and you will be able to make property-based decisions without having to revert to anyone else. Apart from needing your lenders 'consent to let' and informing your insurers that the property is being let, you're pretty much in the driving seat.

---

1. As opposed to 'moveable' or 'portable' property such as goods, materials or vehicles.

'Share of freehold'

You may well come across properties, very often ex-local authority, which have been converted into maisonettes (from the french for 'small house'); one or two-bedrooms upstairs and one or two rooms downstairs. In these cases, it is not uncommon for each leaseholder to own a share of the freehold.

Nowadays, it is possible for individual leaseholders to get together and manage their own affairs. This is achieved by the individuals each owning their own share of the freehold. This is quite common for smaller developments, but the logistics surrounding the management of larger developments make it rather more difficult to do. That said, the property I owned in Dorchester was in quite a significant sized development and the various blocks were all managed by the leaseholders, through their own management company. Associated costs for this sort of arrangement are generally lower than for larger developments. This in part is explained by them being 'non-profit' set ups, although it isn't unusual for the secretary of the company (who invariably does an awful lot of work behind the scenes) to get an honorarium for their time.

Sale of a freehold interest

The leasehold interests described below are all 'carved out' of freehold interests in larger properties owned by someone else, an individual or corporate body. The freehold of, say, a block of flats can be bought and sold, bringing a change of the freehold landlord, and uncertainty. Believe it or not, there are companies and individuals who trade in freeholds. It's possible for your freeholder to change and not necessarily for the better. Regular ground rent income (below), together with various other associated incomes, not least the cost of lease renewals, makes the owning of such freeholds an attractive proposition.

Leasehold

With leasehold properties someone else owns the freehold, usually meaning of a larger block of properties, out of which they grant to you and you buy a long lease ('rights') to occupy the property for a term of years, often as long as 100 years or more. You are effectively renting the property and you never own it in its entirety. What you do own is a leasehold interest in the property that you can then live in or, subject to the terms of the head lease, let to someone else (provided you obtain any consent required by your contract with the free-holder: see later in this chapter). You can also sell your leasehold interest to someone else, or whatever remains of the term.[2]

In practice there are two main varieties of lease depending on whether or not there is a large management company which acts for the freeholder, or a smaller, more intimate management arrangement (of which you may be part). Whichever kind, there will be similar arrangements to what follows and you will make contributions toward the costs associated with the proper running of the development. A development might be anything in size from two mai-sonettes to enormous estates of apartments.

Where there is a large corporate management company

It is not uncommon for a freeholder to arrange for a management company to run its affairs concerning a development. I remain unconvinced that such a management company necessarily works truly for the benefit of the leaseholders. Companies running larger developments, or often several smaller developments, operate in a fundamentally different manner. Whilst they are potentially run in a more professional way, in that they have teams of staff in departments with their own specific responsibilities, they are answerable to their shareholders. They aren't running things in order that costs are kept to a minimum. They are doing it since this is how they earn their livelihoods and pay dividends to their shareholders. These developments may well seem more attractive to ten-ants because they often have additional facilities, such as a concierge service, lifts, a gymnasium, and secure parking. But inevitably, all this comes at a cost.

Ground rent

Historically and under existing leases freeholders have traditionally charged leaseholders a ground rent. A hundred pounds per annum isn't unusual, some-times just a peppercorn rent. However, the terms of leases sometimes allow quite significant increases over time. Clauses allowing a doubling every ten years are not unheard of and this could make an eventual re-sale difficult.

---

2. You may also be able to buy extra years from the freeholder so that it does not become too short to be of real value. There are also what are known as 'short leases' for a lesser number of years and hence (other things being equal) of lower value. See the end of *Chapter 6*.

From 30 June 2022 under the Leasehold Reform (Ground Rent) Act 2022, the Government has abolished new ground rents and outlawed progressively steep existing ones. The provisions also mean that, where ground rents exceed or are set to rise in the future above £1,000 a year in Greater London or £250 elsewhere, the property may by law transition to an assured shorthold tenancy (AST) (*Chapter 18*). One effect is that freeholders have become entitled to gain repossession in the event of a breach of the lease. Unless, that is instead of the AST some fresh arrangement is agreed between the freeholder and leaseholder by variation of the original deed, or due to contracting out of the Housing Act 1988. To clarify, the 2022 Act puts an end to ground rents for most new long residential leasehold properties. The impact of this legislation, which is complex and has 'knock on' effects for existing leases is still emerging, so that this is a topic on which advice concerning up-to-date law and practice is essential.[3]

Insurance

The management company is responsible for ensuring that the fabric of the building has adequate insurance, and this will naturally be passed on to the individual leaseholders in appropriate shares. Where the individual leaseholders control affairs, they can shop around each year to ensure that these and other costs are kept reasonable. Separately, you will be responsible for insuring your contents and liability to your tenants: *Chapter 17*.

Especially if there is a large management company, is it working on a cost-plus basis? Are they receiving a commission from the insurance broker? You may never get to fully-understand the costs associated with these larger companies who often have a reputation for being less than transparent.

Maintenance charges

It is not unusual for smaller management companies to organize a 'sinking fund'. In theory, a budget is determined which considers all the anticipated costs for a period such as communal electricity bills, cleaning, gardening, and a sum towards things such as redecoration, new stairway carpets and minor maintenance. Generally, there is a formula by which these costs are attributed

---

3. See www.gov.uk/government/publications/the-leasehold-reform-ground-rent-act-user-guidance/leasehold-reform-ground-rent-act-2022-guidance-for-leaseholders-landlords-and-managing-agents

to individual leaseholders, to take into account that some apartments are larger than others. We are involved in one such development of 12 apartments where the monthly charges vary between around £50 and £112.

I know of another development of six properties where they all simply contribute as and when bills needs paying. This is perhaps less preferable, since you are always going to be reliant upon individuals being in the position to pay when required. This is especially relevant when you consider that things such as a new roof can easily run to many thousands of pounds. It is surely less painful to contribute an extra £50 a month for several years in advance of a particular expense.

Costs of this kind are likely to be substantially higher in the case of a large management company. Some larger developments also run sinking funds, but I can think of one development in Basingstoke where redecoration costs after ten years came to a significant amount and each leaseholder was presented with an invoice, upon completion, of anywhere between £3,000 and £5,000. This was payable upon demand, in accordance with the terms of their lease.

Additional management costs

Consent to let

Even were you to buy the property off-plan as an investment and even if this is how it was advertised and you were to arrange for a buy-to-let mortgage, you will need to obtain the freeholder's consent to let. Costs vary, but £150 is typical. If you have a change of tenant, that's typically another £150. Even if your tenant stays, you'll be expected to pay an annual renewal fee of maybe £75. And don't forget the VAT.

You might, however, be lucky. I owned two apartments in Swindon and was chased for these fees. When I looked closely at my lease, I realised that it was 'silent' on the matter. This meant that there was no such clause for the company to rely on in trying to make the charge. Others in the same development weren't so lucky. Even though it was silent, it took hours of my time to get them to 'call off their dogs'.

Costs associated with assigning your lease

These are fees which become payable if you sell the property and again tend to be higher with large management companies.

Flat roofs, lifts, concierge, etc.

Having a lift (or in larger blocks several lifts), can be handy. Sadly though, no matter how good they are, they require servicing and repairs. They won't last forever, and it all comes at a cost. Flat roofs have only a limited lifespan and they will also need attending to, sooner or later. A concierge service may well prove to be attractive to tenants, but these people must be paid, and their salaries will only rise over time. Other facilities will come with their own additional costs. The more on offer, the bigger the management company, the more you can expect to have to pay.

Lease length and extension

When a lease is granted, it is granted for a specific period. Lengths vary and the original lease may well have been for a term of anywhere between 99 years and 999 years. When considering a leasehold purchase, ensure that you establish from the outset the length of lease remaining. If you are in your 50s and you have a lease with 60 years remaining, you might think that it won't be a problem. And, if you are paying cash and have nobody to leave it to in your will, then there might not be a problem with this approach. Such a purchase will be consequently cheaper.

A building society or other lender will, however, have an opinion on the length of the lease. Mortgages are being granted for longer and longer terms nowadays and building societies are adopting ever more stringent approaches to leases. They seek to ensure that in the event of default, they have a lease which still has a value. As a rule of thumb, a lender will seek to have at least 35 years on top of the mortgage term. So, if you need a 35-year mortgage, you'll need a minimum 70 years on the lease. And remember, if you do intend to sell it one day, the buyer might need a mortgage term that is longer than you might anticipate today. This is one area where you really must take advice.

A lease may be extended. It's a relatively straightforward matter, although it can be quite costly, and an extension cannot be arranged until the leaseholder has owned a property for two years. A landlord I know added 90 years to each of two leases. One had 63 years remaining and cost him a total of £17,305. The other a total of £18,309. He engaged a professional to conduct the negotiations on his behalf. He is of the opinion that the negotiator's fees represented good value, since proper valuations and negotiations saved over £5,000 per transaction. He paid a matter of several hundred pounds for assistance.

It's worth noting that the shorter the length of the lease that is remaining, the higher will be the cost of the premium. So, as things stand, it's cheaper to do this as early as you can. If you're the chap in his 50s that I mentioned earlier and you intend selling, or leaving the property to someone when you die, it may be worth investigating an early extension. Often when a leasehold property is sold, an extension is sought by the vendor and the work is carried out simultaneously with the conveyancing. It's advisable to get as long an extension as possible and certainly for as long as you can afford.

At the time of writing this, the government is considering changes to leaseholds which may impact upon the ease with which extensions may be granted and the associated costs.

The importance of understanding your lease

Since there are so many potential variations, it is important for you to thoroughly read and understand your lease. It might prohibit the drying of clothes on a balcony, keeping pets or parking in certain places. These are the sort of issues which will irritate you if you are unaware in advance. They are also the cause of sometimes constant friction between occupants.

The lease will detail all the costs I have outlined above and possibly others not mentioned. Whilst a solicitor will highlight any areas of concern, he may assume that you have a degree of understanding of a lease already, so make sure you read it thoroughly and get a complete explanation for all those areas where you require clarification.

Sometimes, you'll discover that fees are payable for alterations made internally. Fancy paying £5,000 for going 'open-plan'? Believe it or not there was a case highlighted recently where one leaseholder was somehow held equally responsible for the alterations made by another. Leases might appear remarkably boring in their content, and it is perhaps tempting to skip through them without concentrating fully. Some clauses look similar to others in the same document or leases you may have experience of elsewhere. Don't be tempted to leave this entirely to your solicitor. Set some time aside to read it carefully without distractions and make notes of, or highlight, every single clause which you are not entirely certain of. And get clarification in writing.

Shared Ownership

As the name suggests, where you buy on a shared ownership basis, you buy a percentage of the property, and the remaining percentage is owned typically by a housing association. You then pay the mortgage on the share you own and rent on the percentage that you do not. You are unable to sub-let under such arrangements, however, so there is no point in considering this sort of purchase for investment purposes.

What Tenure is Best for Investment Purposes?

This will depend entirely upon your own circumstances and the specific terms of any lease being considered. Generally, a freehold proposition means that you are truly in control in every respect, and for most people this is perhaps the preferred option. There are some people, however, for whom a leasehold proposition is fine. The most important thing to take away from this chapter is the need to determine, as early as possible, the exact nature of any lease you are looking at. And to consider all those 'hidden' costs described above which one day will land in your lap. If you aren't entirely happy with your findings, walk away. I'm quite vociferous about large developments with greedy management companies. I had an unfortunate conversation with an investor a couple of years ago which possibly summarises it quite nicely.

The phone crackled after he had been put through and I thought he'd said to me that he was considering investing in a property in a particular development. And I also thought that he was soliciting my opinion. So, I launched into a bit of a rant...

'If you want to buy a property with reduced room sizes as a result of severely sloping roofs that is prone to condensation mould and you're happy with communal areas that stink of cigarette smoke and are full of pushchairs and bicycles, if you don't mind continual and heavy wear and tear to the communal walls and you don't mind fighting over parking spaces, you don't mind cock-roaches and mice, if mattresses being left to rot in the gardens isn't a concern and if for all of this you don't mind ridiculous charges from a management company that really doesn't care, then I think this might be just the investment for you'.

It didn't have a lift though, so apart from top floor tenants having a long stairway with which to contend, it could have been worse in my opinion. Anyway, he didn't reply for a short while. Then he said to me, 'I take it that you don't want to manage it for me then?' It turned out that he wasn't soliciting my opinion, he was looking to engage an agent for managing a tenancy in a property he'd just bought. I fully accept that I didn't handle this call *quite* as well as I might have and that the owner probably didn't wish to deal with someone who was so vehemently opposed to this type of development.

We manage dozens of tenancies in this development, and I would happily have managed his too, it's just that it's an investment I cannot get enthusiastic about. It evaporates a little more with every problem I encounter. If only he'd read a book like this before committing to the purchase!

The Grenfell Effect

Without going into too much detail, suffice it to say that because of the tragic fire in 2017 at a high-rise block of flats in London, other issues have come to light which have proved potentially detrimental to leaseholders. In addition to the much discussed flammable cladding problem, wooden decking, railings to balconies and means of escape in the event of fire have been raised as areas of concern. At the time of writing this book, it is still far from clear who will ultimately be expected to foot the bill for extensive remedial works at affected properties. The Government appears to be willing to fund the bulk of the expenses, but it seems that leaseholders aren't going to get away scot-free.

My Flat in Andover

When I was going through my ill-advised period of lettings acquisitions, I bought a leasehold flat in Andover, Hampshire. It's a large second floor one-bed property situated over commercial premises in a street near the town centre, with all manner of commercial activity in the area. But it's a nice flat and I've only had three tenants since I bought it 17 years ago. Once again, I'll have more to say about this later, but for the purposes of this section it has a lift. Periodically, the lift breaks down. It seems that the freeholder has done a good job of patching things up and of persuading the manufacturer to continue to maintain it, but I recently received an email from him to say that, the next time it breaks down, we'll need to spend £15,000 on it. No doubt when the time comes, that price will have increased. Whilst it is a small development, and it's not run by a huge property management company, there isn't a sinking fund. One day in the not-too-distant future, I'll be presented with a bill for 1/6th of the cost of the repairs. That's £2,500 I'll need to ensure is available at the drop of a hat.

Just for good measure, the property has a flat roof. In around 2014, I had a call from my tenant to say that there was water cascading from a living room ceiling light fitting. It turned out that the flat roof itself was fine, but there were blockages to downpipes. Water collected in deep puddles on the roof and eventually over-ran the lead flashing causing the water ingress. This happened when the freehold was owned by somebody else and their attitude to maintenance wasn't the same as my current freeholder. Somebody's brother was supposed to have attended to deal with it, but a break in the weather disguised the fact that he hadn't. Had it been freehold, I would have had complete control. Had it been part of a large development, it would have been rectified more quickly, but no doubt at far greater expense.

It's perhaps worth noting that in the case of my apartment in a relatively small development, the freeholder runs matters himself and there is no 'greedy' management company or shareholders to keep happy. Such arrangements do exist, although it's also worth remembering that freeholds exchange hands on a regular basis and past performance is not necessarily an indicator of future attitudes and costs.

Conclusion

In my opinion, freehold is best. Next best would be a leasehold of some nature where there is no large management company and where it is lacking in expensive facilities. A maisonette with a peppercorn ground rent and shared responsibilities for repairs would be such an example. An ex-local authority semi which has been converted and the freehold is shared by two leaseholders may also be okay.

Without any doubt whatsoever, walk away immediately from any large commercial conversion which has resulted in dozens or maybe hundreds of apartments, especially if being sold off plan two years in advance, with the aid of sexy brochures and website. One of the largest red flags to beware is the developer offering to guarantee income for a period. I know of a block of apartments sold off plan in 2004 where investors were paid £1,250 per month for several months. As soon as the guaranteed period was over, they realised that this was maybe £400 more than the open market rent. Eighteen years later the apartments still don't achieve £1,250.

I could write a separate book explaining the landlord woes associated with such ill-advised investments. And I am responsible for the management of dozens of investments fitting this description. I really do write with some authority on this matter. And don't forget, I owned a number of these personally. If you *already* own one, I'll merrily manage it for you, but it's likely that your profits are so meagre that you would begrudge every penny of my fees.

CHAPTER 6

Sourcing Your Property

Assuming that you don't already have a property to let (see *Chapter 1*), your first step after deciding to become a landlord will be to locate a suitable one.

Sales Agent

This is probably still the most popular route for the uninitiated. It can be a less stressful way to find and buy a property than searching on your own and it is possible to take your time, with a proper opportunity to discuss and fully consider all the implications. You'll undoubtedly, though, be looking online for something that catches your eye. Major portals such as Rightmove and Zoopla are obvious sources.[1]

Sooner or later, you'll end up in conversation with a sales agent. Try and build some sort of rapport and end up in his 'hot buyers' box. This is often just that, no matter that agents nowadays have sophisticated software, some still have a few cards to flick through, or a book of hot buyers' contact details. Be honest about your financial position and give him a clear definition of the sort of thing you are after. Beware the agent who simply sends you everything on his database. He probably doesn't fully-understand your wants and needs. Have another chat with him. Let him know that you're keen and re-emphasise your aims.

He may have properties that are already being let ('sitting tenants'), which the current owner wishes to sell. These can be convenient in that you already

---

1.   See: www.rightmove.co.uk; www.zoopla.co.uk

know exactly what rent is achievable since the tenant is already paying that amount. Compare this to what is available online through other agents. If a similar property is being advertised for £900 a month and you're told that the tenant is paying more or less than this figure, try and establish why. If a different agent is dealing with that letting, try to find out who it is and have a chat with him as well. It may well be possible for the agent to negotiate an increase in rent, maybe in return for a new tenancy agreement (*Chapter 18*), or perhaps that won't be necessary. Find out, if possible, what the tenant's intentions are. Does he want to stay long-term?

I know of one landlord with a portfolio of around ten properties. He has, over a period transferred them all to us for tenancy management (*Chapter 5*). One was bought several years ago with a tenant who we would both describe as 'less than ideal' and the property is not in the same good condition as the landlord's other properties. It was bought like this, and the landlord had no intention of doing any improvement works until such time as the current tenant left. It is legally compliant in every regard, it's just that it is no longer a particularly appealing place. This might be an appropriate property on which to put forward a bid in certain circumstances whether the tenant leaves or stays. It might be that you decide to make improvements with the existing tenant continuing to live there. But bear in mind the possible disruption to him and I suggest that you don't agree to undertake large projects while trying to work around any tenant. You might find that a sitting tenant has a list of issues he'd like to see addressed. This will almost certainly crop up if you attempt to negotiate a rent increase. It's only by making a few enquiries that you'll get the true picture, so make sure you ask the right questions. Once you know the score you can obviously make your decision and plan accordingly. If your plans affect your likely expenditure, then make an allowance in your offer.

Quite apart from accurately assessing the rental income, by purchasing with a tenant in situ, you won't suffer the costs associated with an immediate void period (*Chapter 3*) and advertising for a tenant. If you are considering a purchase with a tenant in situ, be mindful of the legal and husbandry (i.e. management and care, etc.) issues surrounding the tenancy which are covered elsewhere in this book, and ask for documentary evidence of all the various legal and other requirements that need to be satisfied (*Chapter 22*).

Remember that a sales agent is engaged by his client to simply sell his client's property. There is a fundamental difference in approach to that of a letting agent, who, if he is any good, will give sound advice regarding the long-term potential of a purchase. Out-and-out sales agents rarely have an in-depth understanding of landlord and tenant law niceties, which can lead to other issues. Where the same agent both sells properties and manages a portfolio of tenancies there can be something of a conflict of interest, so make sure that you speak with someone from the lettings department who ought to be better able to distance himself from the vendor's wants and needs.

Below Market Value

Finding a real bargain is undoubtedly what we would all like to do. According to the Royal Institute of Chartered Surveyors (RICS), market value is

> 'the estimated amount for which a property should exchange on the date of valuation between a willing buyer and a willing seller in an arm's length transaction after proper marketing wherein the parties have each acted knowledgeably, prudently and without compulsion.'

Divorce, job loss or financial pressure might easily lead to a sale below market value, to a low offer being accepted. A vendor's desire not to lose out on an onward purchase (in a 'chain') is also a reason for lower offers sometimes being successful. But the advertising of a property at below market value can, perversely, end up in an over market value offer. Since it is human nature to be interested in a bargain, such a property will be spotted by many people who are searching and result in lots of interest. Crowded viewing schedules then create a fear of losing out on something perceived as popular.

I know of properties that have been sold cheaply by building societies simply because of the sums they needed to recover, but mortgagors' repossessions are numerous only when market conditions are dire. I also know of a property sold recently by a developer of 'assisted living' apartments. The way they structured the deal and their desire to sell quickly meant that they sold the property for perhaps £25,000 less than its true worth (around minus 8%). But deals such as this aren't commonplace. Perhaps the last-mentioned sellers had to produce income for their half-yearly figures, or maybe they simply wanted to end their involvement in sales efforts at a particular site.

Nowadays, first-time buyers often save for years to put together a deposit. Only when they are close to having the necessary funds, will they start to look in earnest, but they will have been keeping a weather eye on portals such as Rightmove for some considerable time. You will be in competition with these buyers, but they are not necessarily quite so concerned about getting the property for as little as possible. Cost will be a contributory factor in their decision-making process, but a few thousand here and there won't be the be all and end all. They are also likely to be thinking of their monthly outgoings and savings. Their mortgage payments will probably be less than their rent and getting out from underneath the confines of their existing tenancy agreement will also have value so far as they are concerned. They may have been renting for a considerable time; don't underestimate the sense of empowerment that home ownership can bring and its effect on their thinking when bidding. For a variety of reasons then, it isn't particularly easy to find properties at below market value and demand for them is always going to be high. Please be wary of companies offering easy access to below market value purchases. If the deal is that good, why are they offering it to you? Where is their margin? These middlemen will obviously seek to make a deal look enticing, but it is in their interests to do so.

There was an industry which sprang up in the years running up to the last property crash. It encouraged the unwary investor to buy off-plan and sales companies running effectively an 'introductory service' for the developers. They even charged buyers a percentage for the privilege of encouraging them to purchase over-priced and bad (invariably leasehold) investments. Indeed, it was such a scheme that attracted my business partner and myself all those years ago. Sadly, I've seen some evidence of similar schemes being promoted in the last few years. If you happen to stumble upon a foolproof way of securing properties at below market value, I should be grateful if you would be kind enough to write to me and let me know. In the meantime, consider yourself one of the lucky few if you do somehow manage to get access to such a purchase!

Auctions

There is nothing to stop you considering this route for your first purchase, but in my experience it tends to be less popular for novices. I suspect that it is the speed with which everything happens, the additional risk, and of course not everyone has an auctioneer just up the road. Estate agents, however, are everywhere. TV programmes can make buying at auction look attractive and indeed it can be a good way of obtaining a property. Ensure that you take sensible advice though.

The way an auction proceeds is not the same as with a conventional sale through an estate agent. Make certain that you understand the terms of a particular auction and are able and willing to act quickly in accordance with them. Once the gavel falls, you'll be expected to pay usually a minimum 10% deposit there and then and will have a limited period in which to find the rest of the money and complete the transaction. Failure to do so will expose you to significant financial costs. Before bidding, make sure that you have carried out the usual 'due diligence'. View the property in daylight, take along someone more knowledgeable about it than you if necessary. A property is often at auction because it hasn't sold when marketed in the usual manner. Does it have structural issues? Does it require lots of improvement works? Calculate fully all the costs associated with the purchase and establish the likely rental return in the same way you would were you to take your time and buy through an estate agent. Fix in your mind the highest bid that you can live with and ensure that you don't stray above it.

Don't forget to take a proper look at the legal pack, which will have details of which you absolutely must be aware and fully-understand in advance of bidding. Understand the difference between a guide price and a reserve. Bidding will usually start somewhere around the guide price but will need to meet any reserve placed upon the property by the vendor. Only rarely do properties sell at the guide price and you should expect to pay 10% and sometimes much more over this price. Don't set your heart on getting a bargain simply because the guide price looks attractive to you. It's supposed to have this effect.

Bear in mind that not everybody bidding at an auction will be motivated by property investment. Someone may be bidding strongly purely because of a real desire to live in the place themselves, and may be prepared to pay more than an investor for this reason. And consider also the reckless, naïve or downright stupid investor with seemingly more money than sense. If you have worked out your sums correctly, don't be swayed by others who seemingly know no limit on what they are prepared to bid. Don't be persuaded that they somehow know better than you do. It is far preferable to be upset at having lost out on a deal than to be upset at securing the wrong one. Also, don't forget the auctioneer's premium already mentioned. It will be a percentage of the winning bid and may well add 10% (or more) plus the VAT on that (currently 20%) to the final cost.

Modern-day auctions

These are the online equivalents to conventional auction (where attendees confirm their bids by raising their hands or nodding to the auctioneer as he calls out progressively increasing amounts). Online auctions follow the same procedures but remotely over the internet and against a deadline. Expect fees to be less than those of auctions you attend in person. Note that it is also possible nowadays for online or telephone bidders to compete in a conventional auction, a kind of hybrid arrangement whereby such bids are relayed to the auctioneer 'in the room'.

Short Leases

Other things being equal, buying a leasehold property with a short lease will prove to be cheaper than buying one with a long lease. See particularly the section regarding lease extensions in *Chapter 5*, Tenure.

CHAPTER 7

Yield

Yield is a term which you will see bandied about all over the place during your research. It is important for you to fully-understand what it is. To illustrate this, let's assume that you have four different properties on your radar. They are all differently priced and likely to achieve different rents. You need to have a way of determining which proposition is the best investment. Figure 4 bellow shows different outcomes using simple comparisons.

	Purchase price	Monthly rent	Annual rent	Yield
A	£181,000	£725	£8,700	4.81%
B	£192,500	£950	£11,400	5.92%
C	£251,000	£900	£10,800	4.30%
D	£362,500	£1,100	£13,200	3.64%

Figure 4: Simple price-yield comparison: freehold property

By dividing annual rent by the purchase price and multiplying by 100, you get the yield, expressed as a percentage. In the Figure 4, property B has the best yield at 5.92%. If, however, property B were a leasehold apartment, then you'd have management charges and ground rent to deduct before arriving at net yield. In the Figure 5 below you can see that property B is no longer quite so attractive as it was before consideration of added leasehold costs. What this demonstrates is that the differences in basic yield, whilst illuminating, are sometimes relatively small. If you make a decision based simply upon yield, you are possibly deciding based upon nothing more than a fraction of a percent in returns. Property A is only 0.06% better than Property B.

	Purchase Price	Monthly Rent	Annual Rent	Lease Costs	Yield
A	£181,000	£725	£8,700		4.81%
B	£192,500	£950	£11,400	£2,250	4.75%
C	£251,000	£900	£10,800		4.30%
D	£362,500	£1,100	£13,200		3.64%

Figure 5: Simple comparison of price-yield: leasehold property

When done properly, investing in property will show a healthier return than a deposit account. But whereas the interest rate is generally the only differentiator with a bank account of some sort, in the case of property there are many factors to be considered. The property condition, its location, likely appeal to the rental market and all manner of other things need to be taken into consideration. And there are obviously other costs associated with a purchase. Stamp Duty Land Tax (*Chapter 2*) is one such cost you should consider. Do all your possible purchases fall within the same stamp duty bracket?

Some costs are relatively similar, and you may choose to ignore them. Or alternatively, you may decide to take the spreadsheet to the nth degree and include every possible expense, ending up with a much more accurate analysis. That said, at this stage, there are too many variables and uncertainties to make that sort of detailed exercise particularly worthwhile. Nevertheless, the basic exercise *is* worthwhile and, if you keep it simple, it will quickly demonstrate what an investment is likely to look like in comparison with others you are contemplating.

The chief point of explaining this is to enable you to have one of only a few truly quantifiable reasons to make a particular decision. You won't then be buying a two-bed apartment because you like it, and an agent has said that it will rent easily. You'll be buying the three-bed semi because, based upon your homework, it is a property you like almost as much, it will apparently rent just as easily, but it represents a 1.5% better return than the apartment.

CHAPTER 8

Rental Expectations

I have mentioned income expectations from letting in earlier chapters. It is a subject which has a bearing on innumerable occasions relating to letting property. Let me first explain what I mean by 'rental expectations' and the effect that it can have on cash flow and profitability. Let's say that I have come to see you because you are considering letting your property and you are seeking to engage an agent and solicit the opinion of others regarding rental income. It's a common enough scenario and all agents are asked about this often.

I will have with me a list of comparable properties and the rents that are/ were recently advertised. If you have a three-bed semi in an estate location, I'll bring details of three-bed semis in an estate location. In the case of tenancies I manage, I will be able to show you properties and tell you to the penny how much rent was achieved. I am then able to compare your particular property with those I have brought with me.

To keep it simple, let's say that three in the same road, in similar condition, offering the same facilities, were advertised by a different agent at £925 per month and are now shown as 'Let agreed'. Also, that I had actually let two recently for £900. It is likely that I would be saying to you that £925 is a good price at which to advertise, since that is what the other three were advertised for and, indeed, it might be that the two I let were also at an asking price of £925. I would urge you to give serious consideration to any offer at £900 or above, since I am able to prove £900 has been achieved. There is, sadly, no reliable way of determining what the competitor's properties let for.

Now if you agree with me that £900 is sensible, I'll merrily advertise it at £925 or maybe even £950. Sometimes we get lucky, and the right tenant comes along at the right time. Maybe he's moving from London or somewhere else with high rents and he's over the moon with only having to pay £950. If, however, despite evidence to the contrary, you are determined that your property is worth £1,000, for every month that passes, you'll be £900 out of pocket. If it remains empty for two months, that's a £1,800 loss of revenue in total. You might also be forced to pay standing charges on utilities and council tax.

Letting margins are not really that high and it will take a long time to make up this shortfall, assuming you ever do. Rental expectations are of paramount importance and to try and buck the trend is often folly. As I intimated above, the marketing price isn't necessarily the price at which a property is eventually let, and this is often cause for confusion to a landlord, especially if inexperienced. Were you to ask three agents for a valuation, you might well end up with three different opinions. I'm certain that at least one agent will try and tell you that he is able to get a higher rent than others will. And he may well use this to justify his fees. On occasions, this may be the case, but the majority of the time it is simply an attempt to persuade you to sign up with that particular agent and he might even try and tie you into a 'sole agency' deal for a period of time. Consequently, you might find that it seems as if one agent gets a higher rent, since you will see in the details of comparable properties that you are shown that his are more expensive than others. The point is, however, that the advertised rent might not necessarily be the price achieved. It may be that the landlord has accepted a lower rent for Mr Blue-Chip. It may be that he accepted a lower rent because the tenant was able to move in quickly, thereby saving the costs associated with a void period (*Chapter 3*).

Conversely, it might be that a particular property advertised cheaply is actually let for a higher rent. Let's say that a property is advertised for £1,000, and that the landlord was not prepared to accept a dog living at the property. Someone might have viewed it and suggested paying £1,050 if the landlord would reconsider the prospect of accepting his dog. When a property is sold, the eventual sales price becomes public information and after around three months this information may be collected from the Land Registry or other sources. Perhaps sadly, this information is never available for the rental market. So, no matter for what rent you advertise your property, the pool of potential viewers may negotiate either downwards, or upwards and it's probably best to understand this in advance to avoid the frustration of unexpected offers coming your way.

CHAPTER 9

Tenant Profiles

By my own analysis there are nine (sometimes overlapping) varieties of tenant:

- first-timers
- week-dayers
- long-termers
- students
- sharers
- overseas secondees
- happy tenants
- 'Mr Blue-Chip'
- tenants from hell.

I discuss each of these below and also mention three common situations where restrictions by a landlord can become practical issues. Finally, the chapter looks at finding a tenants, referencing and discrimination.

Unless you wish to attract tenants from a particular demographic, you should base your purchase of a letting (*Chapter 6*) upon the property and its location not your perceived tenant type. I've spoken with many landlords who say that they'd like a non-smoking professional couple with no kids or pets who will agree to a 5% rent increase each year and stay until they retire. They'll pay their rent right on time every month and cause no problems. Strangely enough, I imagine that we would all like tenants like that, but (apart from Mr Blue-Chip who comes close) I think we'd be waiting a long time for them to happen along.

I consider the various tenant types because it is important. Not so that you can necessarily aim for one or more of them, but so you are aware of the kind of individuals you are likely to attract. I believe that you will set out your stall according to your means and your enthusiasm for a given project and will more than likely attract exactly those from the right demographic for your particular property. As I illustrated in *Chapter 3*, letting is not without risk, but the risk can be minimised by tackling matters correctly. When all is said and done, you'll probably end up with the sort of tenants that you deserve. If you offer a sub-standard property, you will likely get a less than ideal tenant. If you offer a lovely property, well-presented and priced, don't be surprised if you quite like your tenants. But I'm now beginning to get into the detail which will help you formulate your plans. I hope the various issues covered in the rest of this chapter will help you to see the sort of tenant you are likely to attract.

1. First-timers

This is a group to which a fair dose of caution needs to be applied. Do you remember the first time you moved away from home? All the excitement that comes with the removal of parental guidance, maybe the prospect of sharing a home with a partner? Let's be honest, it's only the minority of youngsters who have sufficient maturity to be fully-respectful of the terms of a tenancy agreement. Of course, not all first-time tenants are young, but they are certainly less likely to have a full understanding of what living alone, or with a partner, entails. With ourselves for referencing purposes, any tenant under the age of 21 generally requires a guarantor. The guarantor isn't just responsible for the rent if it goes unpaid. He is also responsible for other terms of the tenancy agreement, almost as if living at the property.

I have come across situations where a couple move in together for the first time and within a relatively short period they argue and decide to go their separate ways. It may be that the one who decides to stay put is perfectly able to afford the rent and take over sole responsibility for the tenancy. But, in my experience, it's more likely that the only way the tenancy is affordable is with two incomes. It's usually easier for the tenant with the better income (or best of several) to simply up and move out to somewhere else. I have had to unpick messes caused by break-ups and it invariably leaves a landlord reluctantly having to release his tenant from his tenancy obligations early and allow him to leave. The landlord then has the financial 'penalty' of a void period and all the associated costs. You do, however, need to bear in mind laws preventing you from discriminating because of age. It's perhaps worth noting that insisting on getting a previous landlord's reference isn't this or other discrimination.

When I was 23 years of age

I'd been in the Merchant Navy and just been made redundant. Dave who I had been at college with suffered a similar fate and decided to re-locate to Colchester where I lived at the time. And another friend was looking for somewhere new to live. Consequently, we all ended up in a letting agent's office in a back street near the town centre. A viewing was arranged for later that same day. We all fell in love with a huge property which was in a village a few miles out of town that belonged to a doctor. We told the agent we would take it and were sorting out the finer details: who would have which bedroom, the best part of the garden for the barbecue, who to invite to the housewarming, which of us would get to park where and who'd have use of the garage and its inspection pit.

In 1983, things were a lot different to today in terms of letting property. Fortunately for the doctor, the agent who was finding him a tenant was seemingly as good at her job as the agents I used when I was an accidental landlord and a lucky landlord (*Chapter 1*). We were turned down. And we were furious. But the doctor dodged a bullet.

Our tenants in Preston

Not all landlords fare as well as the doctor from West Bergholt. Unfortunately, those we had at one time in one of our apartments in Preston both worked for the same company which ran into financial difficulties. Both were laid off at the same time. Whilst this wasn't their fault and you might argue that it wasn't foreseeable, it was nonetheless problematic. We had by now parted company with the well-known agent I mentioned earlier and were using a local independent company. The couple were both around 20 years of age and it seems were unable to find gainful employment following their company's demise. Both became dependent on housing benefit. Unbeknown to us, a group of their friends were also made redundant at the same time. They were of a similar age and not all of them had yet left home. Suddenly, still unbeknown to us, our apartment became headquarters for whatever youngsters in this position get up to.

You can probably guess the rest of the story, but the long and the short of it is that, when they finally left, they did so owing rent and with the apartment (which had been immaculate) in utter disarray. They also took with them the security devices for access to the carpark, which cost £100 each to replace. And, as if that wasn't bad enough, some months later we received a communication from the local council informing us that they'd wrongly assessed the tenants' benefits and we owed nearly £1,600 in overpayments!

This cautionary tale has a number of lessons, ranging from being wary about two tenants working at the same possibly unstable company, potentially unsatisfactory referencing, allowing young tenants without guarantors, to engaging the services of an agent without due diligence. And let's not forget the emotive subject of local authorities and their propensity to pay in arrears and then want their money back.

When I suggest that some caution ought to be exercised with first-timers, I suggest this with good reason. This isn't something that I've read in a book or learned from a course. It's something I learned myself and paid the price for.

2. Week-dayers

Week-day tenants or 'week-dayers' are those who stay at their letting during the week and return to their own residence elsewhere (usually) at weekends, where they are often the homeowner. The tenant might have a family and a (possibly large) home in a town that is too far away for a daily commutes and so rents somewhere to sleep Monday to Friday. It may be that his company arranges the tenancy or pays his rent and this can provide peace of mind to a landlord.

Whilst week-dayers are often good tenants, they tend to be short-lived. After all, just how long will someone wish to live apart from his family and put up with the weekly travelling? Invariably, the tenancy ends along with the secondment, or the family relocates, and the tenancy is no longer needed.

I was one once

When my wife and I decided to move back to Winchester, I temporarily rented a one-bed property there. It came complete with a bed, two easy chairs, a pop-up wardrobe, a coffee table, and basic means of cooking. It had electric heating with a meter controlled by the landlord (which cost me a fortune: as an aside, I have subsequently learned that a landlord making money on the supply of electricity is illegal, so beware the temptation).

I absolutely loved my time there and was living the bachelor lifestyle during the week, returning home (or I was sometimes joined in Winchester by my wife) at weekends. I ate out or had takeaways each evening and, when in the property, I was either in bed asleep or watching the TV on my own. I was the 'perfect tenant' and caused no damage or wear and tear whatsoever. I recommend that every landlord have the opportunity of this sort of tenant. Almost without exception, in my experience and that of those whose tenancies I have managed, they are fabulous tenants.

3. Long-termers

This is the sort of tenant that most landlords seek. Quite often it is a young family who move into a home and stay until the children have completed their schooling. You might find that the family gets bigger over time and, assuming the property is large enough, a good landlord might get an eight, or ten year tenancy stay without too much trouble. We have a significant number at between 15 and 20 years in duration.

Long-termers often want to turn your property into their home. Expect requests for consent to decorations that they will offer to do themselves, sometimes at their own expense. You'll possibly end up with Manchester United wallpaper in the boy's room, but so long as the tenancy agreement itself and the terms of any other agreement you come to within it are laid out in writing, you can be reasonably certain of having your property handed back in neutral colours when they leave. Coincidentally, I took on a property in Chineham, near Basingstoke, where the landlord had painted one bedroom wall blue. It ended up being the reason the house let; the young son was a Bristol Rovers fan and I think his opinion carried a lot of sway with his mother!

A potential downside of long-term tenants is that actual rents tend to fall behind market value. For example, my property in Andover is now below market rent, the current tenant having been there for several years. But the tenant is fabulous, treating the place as if she owns it, needing little input from me, and paying the rent on time every month. Another tenant might pay me a higher rent but be 'higher maintenance', or not prepared to stay long-term.

4. Students

This is a specialist area and, in some ways, not for the faint-hearted. Almost by definition, students live in a house in multiple occupation (HMO) Tenancies are arranged around the college year and correct timing is crucial. If you bring a property to this market at the wrong time, you need to be lucky and hope that something has gone wrong elsewhere to find tenants. Since students are not employed and likely to be young, they will all need guarantors which makes for more work, but it usually means that you end up with two guarantors per tenant, each parent jointly and severally guaranteeing the tenancy.

The days when you could offer sub-standard accommodation to students are long gone. Where there is student demand for such properties, there is a lot of competition and the landlords who have the right offerings are the ones who will succeed. There are a significant number of college or university owned blocks being built. This obviously reduces the demand for external private accommodation. If you are considering this market, certainly do some research into the impact of any university-financed housing which might be on the cards.

5. Sharers

Increasingly nowadays, you will need to understand the complexities of HMOs to get involved in more than two sharers. Even where a licence is not required, a growing number of local authorities use 'Article 4 directives' to restrict sharers. An Article 4 directive effectively means that planning permission is required if renting to any more than two people living as a couple, if the other parties are unrelated. Apart from anything else, fire prevention measures need to be put in place. Do take the trouble to look into this if taking on sharers might be of interest. I personally see them most often in modern apartments with two sharing a property with both a family bathroom and an en-suite. Whilst it's possible to let to sharers when there is only one bathroom (and we do occasionally arrange such tenancies) the inconvenience of having to share the bathroom makes such properties less attractive to tenants.

Sometimes, the question of the strength of the relationship is similar to that of the first-timers (above). Indeed, quite often sharers are first-timers themselves. The greater the number of tenants, the more likely there will be some sort of conflict between them resulting in one or more wishing to leave. But, of course, there is far more chance that several tenants will be able, between them, to afford the share of the person who leaves if they don't soon find a replacement for him.

There is the chance of changes of tenants/sharers over time for any number of reasons and it might be that, at the end of a given period, only one of the original tenants remains, with others having joined part way through. Such changes need to be managed for a variety of reasons. First, for your own peace of mind, the occupants need to be named on the tenancy agreement. There is also the question of the deposit. It may be that it was provided in equal shares by the original tenants, so each upon departure will want to get his part back. To do this, each new tenant has to come to an agreement over wear and tear and damages. If a tenant who is leaving has left a burn mark on a carpet, then this needs to be taken into consideration, since at the end of the tenancy you may be seeking recompense from tenants not responsible for the damage.

6. Secondees from overseas

In Basingstoke, there is a large community of IT specialists who work for overseas companies on secondment to UK-based companies and this is undoubtedly true of other towns in the UK. These tenants are usually on relatively short-term contracts, sometimes extended, but a tenancy usually lasts for around 12–18 months. Certainly locally, this is quite a good pool from which to draw. They often land at Heathrow with nothing more than a suitcase or two. Work colleagues point them in the right direction and often they replace a colleague who has just vacated the same property.

They expect fully-furnished accommodation though and care needs to be taken to draw a line beyond which you are not prepared to step in terms of what is included. In my experience and possibly due to differing arrangements in their own country, they sometimes have difficulty differentiating between a tenancy and serviced accommodation (by which I mean that such accommodation is also regularly cleaned, the bedding/towels changed/laundered making it one step away from a hotel minus meals, rather than a conventional letting).

7. 'The Happy Tenant'

I have already referred to my notion of the happy tenant, but it's worth defining exactly what I mean and how it will affect your investment. Having a happy tenant means that your rent is more likely to be paid on time, and your property looked after better than it would have been if he were unhappy And he is likely to stay longer. An unhappy tenant is not likely to match the above criteria.

What makes a tenant unhappy?

Pretty much anything that you do in an unreasonable manner. If you start by treating your tenant in the way you'd expect to be treated were you in his shoes, then assuming you have reasonable standards you shouldn't end up going too far wrong. Let's start with the property itself. Have it presented in good order at the viewing stage and, if you have given any assurances regarding what you intend to do prior to the start of the tenancy then stick to these. If you have stated that you will give the place a clean, tidy the garden or redecorate the living room, then ensure that you fulfil these promises.

I often find myself asking a landlord whether it would have been suitable for him when he was that age and in the same position as his tenant currently is. Would the landlord have happily moved into it? If he wouldn't, then why is he expecting a tenant to? As an aside, if the landlord says that he would but I personally wouldn't, then it's likely that the prospective landlord and I are not on the same page. He's not a like-minded individual and I find myself suggesting that there are other agents better suited to his needs.

A tenant's decision-making process will take into consideration anything that he sees or is promised and if you fail to measure up in some way, then he's going to be upset to a greater or lesser extent. I have lost count of the number of times that a tenant has complained at the start of a tenancy about something which would ordinarily be perfectly acceptable, simply because he has been promised something else and it hasn't come to fruition. Make yourself available or make sure your managing agent does. A growing number of experienced tenants will not entertain a tenancy where there is no agent involved on an ongoing basis. This is because they have experienced landlords who don't answer the telephone, don't return calls and don't respond to emails. Respond fairly and expeditiously to reasonable maintenance requests. Some tenants can be difficult and have unrealistic expectations, but most simply want what they are paying you rent for.

The tenant who wants his lightbulbs changing obviously needs to have his expectations managed and you might need to gently educate him, but the tenant without heating and hot-water has valid expectations that you'll rectify the problem. There are myriad issues for which you have legal obligations (*Chapter 22*), quite apart from moral obligations. Lack of response from a landlord regarding maintenance issues is perhaps the biggest complaint from tenants during a tenancy. There are limits, however, beyond which only the foolhardy will step.

I knew a good landlord who used to pop around periodically and at Christmas he would deliver a hamper. He ended up becoming too friendly with his tenant and this friendship was ultimately abused. His tenant had issues with paying the rent and took advantage of the landlord's better nature. I'm not suggesting that the landlord shouldn't have considered being accommodating of his tenant's circumstances, but try and do this at arm's length. An agent is less likely to fall into this trap since he only earns his keep by the successful collection of rent.

8. 'Mr Blue-Chip'

The blue-chip tenant is someone who:

- is in regular employment;
- is preferably a professional, well paid and respected in his field;
- has a good credit rating;

- understands that he will be credit-checked and referenced (his landlord being prepared to state that he paid his rent on time religiously, every month for some time and was never in arrears);
- looks after the property extraordinarily well;
- doesn't annoy the neighbours;
- never smokes inside the property;
- always respects the property and reports maintenance issues in good time;
- always allows periodic visits and is accommodating of all requests for viewings after he serves his notice to vacate, or when he is served notice because the landlord wishes to sell;
- mows the lawn, tends the flower beds;
- parks considerately;
- his previous landlord was sorry to see leave;
- may or may not be married, have kids or pets;
- will usually find his property through an agent;
- will provide his own deposit;
- will probably want the agent to manage his tenancy, since agents' shops are open five or six days a week and the agents can be checked out;
- understands that for every rogue tenant out there, there is a rogue landlord. (Perhaps he's has a bad experience of this and doesn't want to be reminded of it or get involved in a re-run.)

Be careful with landlord references though. Where possible, take the landlord before last, since if a tenant is a 'tenant from hell' (below), his current landlord will state everything necessary to get rid of his headache.

9. 'The Tenant from Hell'

This is the polar opposite of Mr Blue-Chip. He:

- won't pass referencing or credit-checks;
- has a chequered employment history;

- has experienced a series of bad landlords and got away with pulling every stroke imaginable in retaliation. He now doesn't give a hoot, so long as he has somewhere to hang his hat;
- realised years ago, that no respectable agent will consider him and so he preys on the desperate landlord, or the landlord who doesn't care. He knows where to find these landlords: shop windows, through mates of mates, Gumtree, Facebook, or similar websites;
- is sometimes charming and sometimes entirely believable;
- understands the rights of tenants and knows that, once he has a tenancy agreement, he is safe until the bailiffs turn up. He knows this because, for advice, he turned to the local council and Citizen's Advice Bureau years ago;
- doesn't have two pennies to rub together, and knows that it doesn't matter how he treats a property. After all, you can't get blood out of a stone. Besides, it's probably a council bond and not his own deposit.

Restrictions

The following are amongst the more common tenancy restrictions you are likely to encounter and you may therefore need to deal with their impact. Often the basic restriction is weaved within the tenancy agreement but equally and subject to what the freeholder's head lease dictates, there may be provision in the tenancy for that reason. Often both head leases and tenancy agreements may allow variation of some restrictions by (usually) written consent.

Pets

Some 40% of the population have pets of some description. Saying no to dogs or cats will hinder your search for tenants. Saying yes, with conditions, will significantly increase your ability to let at the best price and expediently. Most leasehold apartments will have terms in the freeholder's head lease which prohibit cats and dogs, but then most of those with pets aren't looking to live in apartments.

I would go so far as to state that a tenant with a pet is less likely to haggle over the rent since he understands that fewer landlords will accept a pet. Since the tenant fee ban (*Chapter 21*), whereby deposits have been limited to five weeks' rent, even more landlords have decided not to accept a tenant who has a cat or a dog. Before the ban, he could have demanded a higher deposit which provided at least some peace of mind. Post-tenant fee ban, however, he can no longer do this. But were he to accept a pet and charge a higher rent, which isn't refundable like a deposit, he would actually be better off. I believe that a rent of perhaps 5% more (in effect a surcharge) is usually achievable. Don't make it £x without pet or £y with a pet though, as this can have unintended consequences when, e.g. the dog dies. Simply increase the rent and only be prepared to renegotiate with someone without a pet.

If you do decide to accept pets, remember to state in your adverts that you are prepared to do so. You will be in the minority and stand out from the majority A half-hearted attempt at encouraging landlords to accept pets is being made by the Government,[1] but a landlord is still usually able to avoid having to take such tenants. However, you cannot easily refuse a tenancy to someone with an assistance dog, such as those whose sight is impaired. You can, however, be almost certain that the trained dog is unlikely to cause damage.

Children

Some landlords are reticent to accept children. By and large, this is self-defeating since many homes on the market are attractive to those with children or considering starting a family. There are, however, occasions when I don't personally have too much of a problem with this stance. We have the landlord of a 6th floor apartment with a balcony who has decided that he doesn't want the risk of a young child falling from it.

Fires and other risky activities

Tenancy agreements frequently forbid risky activities on the property or permit manageable hazards after obtaining the written consent of the landlord. It is always wise to take specialist advice if you are concerned (as well as checking your insurance policy: *Chapter 17*).

---

1.   The White Paper 'A Fairer Private Rental Sector' is mentioned in *Chapter 22*.

Referencing

The satisfactory referencing of tenants is mentioned many times in this book. Referencing has two distinct aspects, financial and personal, Using credit referencing agencies you or your agent will want to know that the applicant can readily afford the rent allowing for a safe margin and the vagaries of the economy. But you will also wish to know from his previous landlord or referees that he is the type of person whom you can trust to look after your property (like Mr Blue-Chip above), and additionally for the purposes of any insurance that you take out (*Chapter 17*). See also especially, *Chapter 21*, Deposits.

Finding a Tenant

It usually takes a few weeks to find a tenant and for that tenant to move in. It is possible to find tenants who are looking for an immediate start to tenancy, but most tenants plan ahead. They are looking because they have been served a Section 21 notice (*Chapter 22*), in which case they were given at least two months' notice, or they are about to serve notice themselves, in which case they will need to give at least a month's notice at their existing home, probably having to coincide with their rent due date.

If your potential tenant has been legitimately served less notice, then be wary. Notice periods for having damaged a property or for anti-social behaviour are shorter. Overall, this usually means that it might be longer than you really want before he is able to start a tenancy. Most tenants would rather not have two lots of rent to pay.

If for some reason, you are desperate to move a tenant in then this is something you will need to manage. If money is the issue, then it may be that you need to look at the structure of your investment. For if money is tight before a tenant moves in, what is going to happen when you have a boiler break-down or some other costly repairs with which to deal?

Use the time constructively and carry out some of those little jobs that you haven't got around to completing. Anything that will make your tenant's home better will go down well. Of course, let's not forget that you could find a tenant through word-of-mouth, on Facebook, Gumtree or something similar. I dare say that it would be easy to find a tenant, were you determined enough. The problem with this, in my experience, is that it's not where blue-chip tenants find their next home. And it's them to whom you should be attracted.

Discrimination

A landlord must not discriminate, including on any of the following grounds (noted alphabetically but all of equal importance). He may otherwise risk criminal sanctions (see generally *Chapter 22*):

- age;
- disability;
- family status;[2]
- gender;
- marital status;
- race;
- religion;
- sexual orientation.

A significant proportion of landlords are reticent to let to applicants in receipt of housing benefit. For some, it is simply a case that their insurance or mortgage terms prevent them from doing so. Insurers and lenders are now having to change their stance to this restriction. This is because it has been deemed to discriminate against single mothers. Landlords must now be careful when exercising their right not to agree to a tenancy. You are no longer able to put a disclaimer on an advert which bans applications from those in receipt of benefits.

---

2.   For example, if the tenant is a parent/carer of a child over 18 or of someone with a disability.

CHAPTER 10

How Big?

Assuming you don't already have somewhere to rent out, this chapter deals with the question 'What size of investment property is best?' I also give an indication of the likely length of tenancies geared to the size of the property. This is based upon around 3,200 tenancies over my years as an agent. Whilst you should conduct your own research to discover the likely length in your local area, this should give you a steer. At the end of the chapter Figure 1 shows a typical daily total for properties in Basingstoke being marketed on Rightmove. No doubt there will be variations in your own area, nonetheless, I believe it is indicative of the relative number of each property type available on any given day. You can easily establish demand at Rightmove's website.[1]

Annexes and Studios

Smaller annexes and studios (the latter often based around one large living/sleeping-equipped room) are most often taken by shorter-term tenants with an average tenancy length of 12 months. It might be a 'week-dayer' or a first-timer (see *Chapter 9* for both), someone on a budget, or simply who is seeking to minimise outgoings. There are exceptions to every rule, and I dare say that readers will have heard of someone who has lived in a studio for years. But in my experience, such tenancies are short-lived. What this means to a landlord is that he will suffer more regular void periods than with larger properties. Even if a property is let in quick order, it is never good practice to move one

---

1.   See: www.rightmove.co.uk

tenant out on the Friday and another in on the Saturday. If you want to attract my 'happy tenant' (*Chapter 9*), then he'll wish to move into a property that is genuinely clean and tidy and without minor maintenance issues that should have been dealt with between tenancies.

No matter how you source your tenants, there will be associated costs. Even if you find your tenant free of charge on Facebook or somewhere similar, you should allow adequate time to conduct viewings, take up references, draw up the agreement, lodge the deposit, update/check the inventory, notify the council and utility companies, etc. One aspect of a change of tenancies that is often overlooked is the need for a tenant to move furniture in and out. Smaller properties such as studios still need beds and other large pieces of furniture and there are invariably small knocks to walls and door frames. Irrespective of whether you make a deduction from the deposit of the outgoing tenant for such damage, it increases the amount of work that you need to carry out to bring the property back up to scratch. So, if you change tenants every six months, you're going to have twice the potential for such damage if it turns out to be less than my suggested 12 months average tenancy. Nonetheless, it might be that a studio is all that may be purchased within your budget. That's fine, just make sure that you take into consideration these issues when making your plans. I say more about annexes in *Chapter 11*.

One-bed Apartments/Houses/Maisonettes

Tenancy lengths for apartments tend to be 24 months, for houses 19 months. It might be argued that these two property types attract different kinds of tenant. To an extent that's true. But in my experience many applicants for them make contact simply because they need somewhere to live, and these are both within their budget. Indeed, the same tenant may have considered a studio (above).

The one-bed tenant is unlikely to have children to consider and, if a garden is included, then maybe it will prove to be a pleasant bonus when the weather is right, but some tenants will regard it as a chore. The tenant here is still likely to be a first-timer, week-dayer or someone on secondment (*Chapter 9*). Without over-simplifying matters, with first-timers these tenancies tend to last until they outgrow the property. A tenancy for a large one-bed property is likely to last longer than a small one-bed, simply because it takes longer for the lack of storage space to become an issue. Another driver behind a tenancy ending is two people outgrowing a one-bed property. Often a single person meets a partner after which they wish to move in together. All of a sudden, that storage issue has doubled, and the tenant starts looking for a two-bed property.

As a rule, a landlord with a one-bed apartment is competing with considerably more apartments than landlords with other homes. This is simply because so many are being built and offices are being converted to apartments. The quality of most newly built or newly converted properties also tends to be higher than those of a few years ago. So, whilst the target tenant is arguably the same, that tenant will have a selection of similar properties from which to choose. Don't forget that this target tenant often doesn't mind whether he lives in a flat or a house, so the fact that you have fewer one-bed houses to compete with doesn't mean that you have less overall competition.

Two-bed Apartments/Houses

Here the length of tenancy is likely to be as follows: apartments, 19 months; houses, 24 months. These properties are often still of appeal to the same type tenants as I have already described above. That said, it's more likely that parking spaces and gardens will begin to become a factor. It may be that a first-timer or a week-dayer (*Chapter 9*) will look at these, but the rent is likely to be a bigger consideration to these two groups of would-be tenants. Such properties are also often the target for those on secondment from overseas. Frequently a single individual starts the tenancy, but with the express intention of being joined by their partner within the foreseeable future. And often there's a small child or two in the equation as well. A pair of professional sharers will also be looking at this sort of property, especially if it has an en-suite bathroom

The owner of a two-bed house or apartment is in the same boat in terms of competition as the owner of the one-bed. There are many two-bed houses, but there are generally far more two-bed apartments to rent at any one time.

Three-bed Houses

Generally, three-bed apartments aren't common, so I will not give a lot of consideration to them. Yes, there will be a demand, but it will be rather less than for other properties and I suspect with lesser yields (*Chapter 7*). If you already own such a property, you will certainly find a tenant, but if you are considering purchasing one, you would be well-advised to do some research including into whether a three-bed house (where the average tenancy length is 31 months) would be better and speak with local agents. In 2022, the average UK household has 2.9 bedrooms, which makes the three-bed house a particularly tempting proposition for the investor. This is the favoured property of the long-termer and the sort to which an investor should, in longevity terms, aspire. New house sizes in 2022 are some 20% smaller than in the 1970s. Land is more expensive than ever, building costs are significantly higher than they were and one of the ways in which we can all be encouraged to buy property is to make them as affordable as possible. The simplest way of achieving this is by making them smaller.

In the lettings market demand for three-bed, ex-local authority housing is very good indeed, since homes built by councils in the 1970s are of sensible proportions. They have a reasonable garden, possibly a garage and, assuming they have been refurbished over the intervening years, double-glazing and gas-fired, radiator central heating. Of course, the same may be said for three-bed homes privately built in the same period. It may well be that you are able to find one and it will be just as well-suited to the task. With it having been privately owned for the duration, however, there's a lot more chance that it has received rather more in the way of extensions, a conservatory, etc. and it may therefore be that much more expensive.

One of the ironies of letting is that a higher purchase price doesn't necessarily mean a higher rent. There are examples of properties in every city, town or village which are seemingly identical, but which are situated in different areas in terms of desirability. The more desirable might fetch an extra 5%- 10% were it to be sold, but it might be that you can walk into town or to school from a less desirable area, and that might make it easier to let it at a higher rent.

Beware the three-bed property which is identical in footprint size to the two-bed neighbour. When local authorities used to build houses, they would have a selection of two-bed and three-bed properties which were identical downstairs, varying only in the sub-division of space upstairs to create an extra bedroom. The latter were handy for families with small children but instead of two true double bedrooms they ended up with one true double for mum and dad, one reasonable sized room for maybe two kids sharing and one small bedroom for the youngest. Builders in the private market have adopted the same approach, no doubt because a three-bed will sell for more than a two-bed. I can think of examples where the rent for a three-bed is not much more than that of the two-bed with the same overall dimensions. And there have been occasions where it was in fact lower.

Four-bed (Plus) Houses

In my experience, the feasibility of a letting proposition tapers off as the size of the property increases. Certainly, in terms of yield, a multi-million-pound property will be less fruitful and far more difficult to find a tenant for. At the extreme high end of the market, there simply isn't much demand at all (unless maybe you are in unusually upmarket locations or money no object). This said, a four or five-bed property doesn't necessarily make for a bad investment and once again, if you already own one, it will likely rent without difficulty.

There is no such thing as an average tenant in the same way there is no such thing as an average landlord. However, we are all constrained by income and usually seek to be sensible in disposing of it. Quite simply, anyone able to afford the sort of rent which would be demanded of a four-bed property is more likely to be able to buy one of his own. There are individuals who get relocated by their companies who do offer packages which often include covering the cost of renting property. These perks, however, are seen less often and, where they do exist, they are for rather limited periods of time.

Owing to the smaller yields, relatively short tenancy lengths and comparative lack of demand, a landlord would be well-advised to think long and hard before buying too large a property for investment. There may of course be other factors influencing the decision. You might be hoping for planning consent, you might one day wish to move in yourself, or you might see the potential of buying a run-down example and improving it. But otherwise, larger properties aren't necessarily such a good proposition.

Changing Properties in Order to Let

Every now and then, a landlord will come to see me to discuss letting a property which, owing to its size, value, sometimes location, and often the landlord's circumstances, isn't an ideal rental prospect. It might be a lovely well-presented property, but for whatever reason the overall deal simply isn't attractive.

Prior to investing in letting, consideration of all the alternatives is a must. For example, I came across a house which had been inherited that had been occupied by elderly relatives for an extended period. It might have required tens of thousands of pounds in expenditure to make it attractive enough to let. The owner would have needed to spend a considerable sum on double-glazing, a new boiler, new carpets, redecoration and maybe a new kitchen or bathroom, so the decision to sell and re-invest was made easier. A smaller, more modern, and compact property was an obvious replacement for investment purposes. I say some more about property types, their merits and demerits in *Chapter 11*.

Property type	Available
Studio	9
1 bed flat	64
1 bed house	9
2 bed flat	84
2 bed house	19
3 bed flat	1
3 bed house	32
4+ bed house	12

Figure 6: Property types available to rent: One day in Basingstoke

More on Property Types: Merits and Demerits

Having outlined the main differences between *leasehold* and *freehold* properties in *Chapter 5* which deals with Tenure and various *sizes* of rental properties in *Chapter 10*, How Big? this chapter considers further aspects of their merits and demerits for prospective investors as well as some additional perspectives.

More About Annexes

By annex I mean a lesser part of a property that is joined to or associated with the main premises containing space that can be rented out. Annexes vary significantly. We manage tenancies in around ten such properties and no two are similar. Some are truly self-contained, others simply a suite of rooms let under a lodging arrangement with the landlord sharing facilities. They may be conversions within an existing property, sometimes separate but close to it. They may or may not have a separate access. I can't think of anyone I know who has bought an annex as such by way of investment. If you have space for one, suffice it to say that you'll need to take advice, since the type of tenancy agreement you use will depend upon your exact circumstances. You will, however, still need to adhere to legislation concerning deposits, legionella risk-assessments, gas safety, electrical safety, the right to rent and other areas of landlord and tenant law (see *Chapter 22*).

Studios/Flats/Maisonettes/Apartments

I have bracketed these together for the purposes of this chapter since their merits and demerits are similar. Having explained in *Chapter 10* that they tend to be let to the same sort of tenant, let's consider some further issues.

My 'Happy Tenant' crops up here, possibly more so than anyone else. He is now living near other people so may not be quite so happy as he once was. Some of these people, like him, will be tenants, and some may be owner occupiers. This is an important distinction, and rather like oil and water, they don't always mix well. I've already mentioned a development of 12 apartments where we are partially involved in the management of the block. This has meant that we have been obliged to deal with both owner-occupiers and tenants when in dispute. At the petty end these can manifest in complaints about cardboard boxes not being crushed before being put in the bin store. But they can easily escalate to those about people parking inconsiderately, slamming communal doors late at night, loud music being played at all hours, cigarette smoke wafting into shared areas, soiled nappies left in hallways, cars being vandalised, tyres slashed, offensive notices being displayed in windows, washing machines that are too noisy, and neighbours clinking their shoes on laminate flooring. The list of grievances seems endless.

It is not always the tenant who is the cause of the problem, sometimes they are on the receiving end, but these things can take up an inordinate amount of management time. In the block I've mentioned, three agents are involved, together with a self-managing landlord, and the approach of each is different. General disharmony is not unusual in these circumstances. My formerly quite happy tenant begins to wonder about moving elsewhere because of issues with neighbours. I can think of three who have vacated what should have been a pleasant place in which to live. That's three unnecessary void periods, three fresh set up costs and three lots of minor wear and tear issues to deal with. And it's such a shame because the block is otherwise managed well by a number of leaseholders who have bought the freehold and been trouble-free in terms of maintenance. Ordinarily it would be an example of the sort of place I wouldn't sneer at suggesting to an investor. There's no greedy management company, no expensive concierge service, no lift, or flat roof issues. That said, dozens of our tenants live in apartments close to a railway station, town centre and other amenities, and most of them live happily and in complete harmony. That one temporarily troublesome block isn't necessarily a shining example of this sort of investment.

Upstairs or Downstairs?

I am often presented with a choice between two flats: one upstairs and one downstairs. They are seemingly identical and yet, all else being equal, I would take the downstairs one every time. Generally, there is direct access to the garden from a ground floor flat and this has benefits. Barbecues in the summer, somewhere for the kids to kick a ball about, etc. By comparison, the upstairs flat has no easy access to outside. The tenant has to go downstairs, locking his front door before walking around the garden of the downstairs flat to reach his own behind it. So his garden is hardly used and looking after it becomes a chore. No matter how hard you try as a landlord, that garden will invariably look scruffy. It certainly won't help to let the property in the same way patio doors onto a nice, secluded garden will.

Don't panic about a flat being on the ground floor. For every tenant who dislikes the prospect of ground floor bedrooms there is another with mobility issues, or who doesn't like carrying shopping up staircases, or appreciates convenient garden access. And these premises are often somewhat cheaper.

What is clear about these offerings is that a fair amount of research into the exact nature of the proposition would be required were a landlord to be considering them. There is as you can see a lot more than simply the purchase price to think about.

Terraced or Semi-detached?

There are clear advantages and disadvantages to both propositions. Don't let your own preferences cloud your judgement. Personally, you might be used to living in a detached property and you can't even imagine how anyone could possibly live in a terraced or semi-detached home. But assuming this is an investment, you won't be living there, so your thoughts on what the property is like in this regard are somewhat irrelevant. For an individual accustomed to living in a single room in a shared house, or who is used to the confines of a flat, it will be a step up the ladder. Or it might be exactly what they have always lived in. It might be handy for a school, family, friends, or work. It might be their idea of a 'forever' home. It might be the quaint garden or the view that has sold them on it.

As an investment, it might be that purchasing an end-of-terrace or semi-detached house gives you the potential to apply for planning consent and one-day extend, or even build another house on the plot. I know of several landlords who've succeeded in doing this. Ignore for the minute the yield from rent or the capital appreciation on the original property. They have all added tens of thousands of pounds to their portfolio simply by buying a property with development potential.

The running costs associated with terraced properties are undoubtedly less than those of a detached or semi-detached property. Your neighbours kindly help in the heating of your home. In terms of maintenance, you have less roofing, guttering, soffits and fascias to worry about and usually fewer windows. There is undoubtedly the noise consideration from two sides to be borne in mind, but an occupant will probably have a greater sense of personal security which is important, e.g. for the elderly or otherwise vulnerable.

Don't forget also, the character which so often comes with these properties. Thirty years ago, I owned a Victorian semi-detached property with a fireplace that was practically an inglenook. It had a bay window with a view right down the road and a garden that abutted a canal tow path. For me, at least, this made it more desirable than others in the same street. We manage several tenancies in a variety of locations in properties with such character. There is an element of the tenant population who will merrily pay more for such features. You might almost say, the more features the better: claw-foot baths, log-burners, Aga cookers, stripped floors, exposed brickwork, etc. Okay, so not all such properties have these, but even one or two elements may prove desirable to potential tenants.

If we consider property size once again, modern terraced properties and semi-detached houses are not as large as those of the 1970s or earlier. And size will often be important to your tenant. Of course, not all such properties are going to be everyone's idea of a dream home. Be sure to consider all manner of other issues which you might easily overlook or think unimportant. As emphasised elsewhere in this book, *you* won't be living in the property, but you do need to think about the potential problems associated with living there. Would you want a bus stop outside your living room window, streetlights shining into the bedroom, or a steep hill with which to contend when the parking is some way down the road? How about your wheelie bins and those of your neighbours parked up against your wall all day, every day? Why buy a potentially hard to let property when you can take your time and buy something free of such issues?

Detached Properties

I'm sure that for most tenants this would be their preferred choice. I know some who would consider nothing else. If there is a caveat, it is to consider the garden size. I look at gardens later in this book (see *Chapter 13*) but suffice it to say here that generally speaking and as a landlord/investor you don't want too large a garden. By the same token someone renting a detached property is expecting to get something in proportion to its size. There are obviously exceptions to every rule, but you do need to consider the tenant's reaction to being hemmed in or alternatively having to contend with acres of land.

Character Properties

I've already mentioned the character of some older properties. By 'character' in this section, I mean a quaint thatched cottage with roses growing over the door, or perhaps a one-time gatehouse to a country estate, or something similarly unusual. It might be detached, although not necessarily, and it might have any number of rooms.

Fabulous though they may be to admire or live in, as investment propositions they are rarely going to stack up. If you already own one, then it will be entirely possible to let it, but unless there is a compelling reason to buy something 'out of the ordinary', it probably shouldn't appear on your list of target properties.

CHAPTER 12

Location

If you originally bought a home to live in, the reason you chose it was partly on emotional grounds. And this driver won't necessarily translate into making it desirable to a prospective tenant. That said, some of your grounds for buying might have been practical ones which makes some of your thought processes transferable to letting. School catchment areas being a good example of something a potential tenant may find appealing. If you found the street convenient with lots of free parking, then so will tenants.

Of course, not all first time landlords are using a property that they originally lived in. There are two fundamental errors made by a novice investor. One is by the landlord who tells me 'I'm interested in buying in this particular area because I like it/I live there/I would prefer it myself'. Or conversely, 'I don't want to buy in this particular area because I don't like it/I wouldn't want to live there'. These point to an investor not being on the right page (*Chapter 1*). Even if the area is suited to letting, the landlord needs to understand that it's suited for reasons other than whether or not he 'likes it'. Remember from what I said before that my suggestion is to make decisions in as dispassionate a manner as possible. This is a clear example of where you need to step back from your own prejudices.

Local Facilities

Your *property must be right* to attract *the right tenants* vis-à-vis local facilities such as shops, a pub, a theatre, gym or swimming pool. For example, investing in a one-bed flat in a village location won't necessarily be as successful as investing in the same flat in town. There is a village where we let three- and four-bedroom homes without too much difficulty. It is only four miles from Basingstoke centre, but it still has shops, pubs, a school, a butcher, and a café. In short, it is a perfectly nice place to raise a family and for the right property it can be more expensive than in town. We manage several tenancies comprising one-bed flats in this village. There is nothing wrong with the flats; they are generally well looked after, have plenty of parking and there is a nice community feel about the place. Sadly though, we invariably take longer to let them than their equivalents in town. And they achieve probably 7% less in rent. This is at least in part because the sort of tenants who live in one-bed flats are often single, or young couples, and socialising may be more important to them than it might be for a family. The nightlife in Basingstoke is a draw, especially to the younger generation, but the cost of taxis or not being able to drink and drive if you live 'out of town' is sufficient to make a remote flat less attractive.

Population

The village I've mentioned has a population of around 5,500. Were the same property to be advertised in another village which is a similar distance from Basingstoke, but with a population of less than 800, I suspect that the problem would be even worse. It might be that a tenant could be found, but he would likely be from a very specific demographic, and they are undoubtedly far more thin on the ground.

Schools

It's not always possible to buy an investment property within the catchment area of a popular and a highly regarded school, but the draw cannot be over-emphasised. And if you're buying a family property, this is a consideration. Were we to advertise two identical properties, one within such a catchment area and one just outside of it, the one within the area would go more quickly and undoubtedly at a higher rent. We have several schools which are frequently mentioned by prospective tenants. A poor teaching reputation or adverse reports obviously has the opposite effect but it is equally important to check this out.

Risk of Flooding

Insurance against the risk of flooding is becoming problematic, especially in those areas with a recent history of this. I have had to contend with the fallout from two floods in recent years caused by riverbanks bursting. It never ceases to amaze me that builders continue to construct and sell properties on low-lying ground around rivers. These might be fabulous places when the sun is shining but, for whatever reason, major incidents seem to be happening far more frequently than was once the case. In my own village, flooding was caused not by a river bursting, but by torrential rain running off already sodden ground and the drains not being able to cope with the volume of water from sustained downpours.

Unlike local councils and housing associations, private landlords aren't responsible for the costs associated with re-homing their tenants once a property is uninhabitable but, in the event of a flood, will have significant damage with which to contend and the danger of not being able to secure insurance afterwards. You can carry out searches to assess the risk of flooding if you are in any doubt. And of course, a local agent ought to be able to advise.

Shops, Pubs and Entertainment

There are two ways of looking at proximity (or otherwise) to shopping and recreational facilities. On the one hand, shops and pubs are in varying degrees necessary and welcome. The villages mentioned above both have shops and pubs and I know that all are frequented and supported by their local communities. There is no need to jump in a car or catch a bus on those occasions when you need a pint of milk, a newspaper or a pint of beer. And, where it is relatively easy to walk to a local superstore of some description it is most definitely a selling point.

There are several large housing estates in and around Basingstoke with parades of shops, takeaways, petrol stations, etc. But not all shops are the same. There are a few roads I would steer clear of entirely, one or two where the wrong end of the road could from what I see and hear be troublesome. Youngsters have a habit of congregating around chip shops, kebab houses, etc. and noise and other issues are not uncommon. If your tenant finds getting to sleep difficult, or feels intimidated when doing his shopping, he probably won't stay long. Why leave yourself open to problems associated with letting a property, which tenants might suffer?

My flat in Andover

As I explained in *Chapter 5,* my Andover flat is a lovely and large property with a fabulous tenant. I also mentioned that it was situated over commercial premises in a road near the town centre. Almost opposite is a kebab shop. There are two pubs within a few yards and no end of other shops and offices. For good measure, there is — or was last time I was there — a comedy club a few yards up the road. Oh, and I might as well mention that no tenant with a car is going to be interested, since there's no parking. I have been remarkably lucky with this and other investments but, were an investor to speak with me regarding such a proposition, I really would urge caution, despite my good fortune.

Trains, Buses and Taxis

An assumption frequently made by investors is that if they buy near the railway station they will attract tenants who commute by train and don't need a car. Lots of our tenants living near the station do not commute. Whilst some don't have cars, they tend to be the exception nowadays. The conclusion to be drawn from this is that you must be sensible about the likelihood of your tenants needing or wanting parking space (see next section). If you assume that they won't need parking, you are probably limiting the appeal of your investment.

Closeness to transport may prove to be double-edged swords. It's handy to have a railway station, bus stop or taxi rank nearby, but not so handy if it's on a busy route and a popular place for hordes of noisy commuters.

Parking

If not the single most important issue, lack of parking is certainly right up there with the best of reasons why a tenant will choose not to rent a property. In Basingstoke, there are places with on-street parking only. Tenants may apply for a resident's permit plus a spare visitor's permit for a relatively modest annual fee. This allows them to park outside their property or in five or six neighbouring streets. What this means though is that a tenant isn't guaranteed to find a parking space which is wholly convenient. Shopping trips become far more of a challenge when you need to park 600 yards away.

In most towns some residential streets were built before we had cars. Even those constructed in the 1960s which I've been raving about for other reasons were designed for far fewer cars than we have nowadays. Blocks of apartments with just one space per apartment are not uncommon, some with few or no visitor spaces. Some tenants have two cars and larger families with young adults might have three or more. I've encountered several instances where parking disputes got out of hand. One landlord of ours with a property built in around 2006, which came with a parking space, felt obliged to have a post installed which the tenant must lock in position each time he leaves, just so that he can ensure the space remains free upon his return. He pays a lot of rent to live in a house with a parking space and yet must suffer the discomfort of getting soaked every time it rains, just because of the additional time taken to deal with his post.

The block to which I referred earlier where there have been inter-occupant disputes was where we also had 'parking rage'. Unfortunately, it ended with slashed tyres and scratched bodywork. Ironically, it wasn't just the occupants of the block who were involved. Since the development had been unoccupied for some considerable time, other residents in the street had become accustomed to parking there.

My apartments in Preston again
We paid extra for spaces for each of our apartments in a secure car park (for which access was gained using £100 a time key fobs!). Ironically, we were to learn that few of our tenants had vehicles and we could have saved ourselves this cost. But I'm convinced that this is an example where events would have

conspired against us had we not bought parking spaces. Each potential tenant would have turned a tenancy down because of the lack of parking!

Access to the National Road Network

Imagine that you have the choice of living in two or three different properties. They are equally appealing in most respects; handy for the shops, have off-road parking and good schooling. If one is three minutes from a main arterial road or motorway and the other is down a warren of side roads with traffic lights and you work a 45-minute drive away, which would you take? Some tenants I speak with are couples, each working in towns other than Basingstoke. They have settled on the town because it is central for the two of them, wanting it to be as convenient as possible with good roads to both workplaces.

Conclusion

I've given examples of the sort of reasons why a particular location might be suited or unsuited to someone and a few thoughts on why somewhere might be more, or less, ideal for them. This is thrown into the mix to illustrate that you cannot be all things to all prospective tenants and all I say in this chapter must be considered in the context of the 'Covid-19 revolution' where working from home at least part of the time has changed some individuals' aspirations, travel needs and demands (such as a good internet connection). Ultimately, you have no real idea of the sort of individual who is going to be attracted to your property, other than I believe that you reap what you sow. You'll attract a like-minded individual for whom the location is right, or for whom the compromises are acceptable. It is worth bearing all of what I say in mind when considering a purchase but also try not to get too wrapped up in it. Buy a sensible property, present it well, and manage your expectations—and you'll find you get tenants.

CHAPTER 13

The Property Itself

I hope you will find this chapter contains much sensible, practical advice. It looks at furnished and unfurnished lettings, décor, and how best to prepare and equip different rooms for your tenants. If you don't yet have the property, it is vitally important to conduct thorough research bearing such things in mind, as well as studying the local market before choosing something appropriate for you. Look at a variety of properties, even if you have no intention of buying them. This will give valuable insight into what else is available. Get a real idea of the quality of properties on the market. Kitchens and bathrooms which I deal with later in the chapter merit particular attention.

Some of the properties you view will be bought by other investors who, in effect, are your competitors. Speak to a letting agent and ask to see some of his properties, to understand what good, bad and indifferent landlords have on offer. If you find some resistance from agents in this regard, that's good. It will help you compile a list of those with whom you might or might not like to deal on an ongoing basis.

The quality of the average property on the market is significantly higher than it was even a decade ago. Rents have increased significantly, and tenants nowadays have higher expectations. Whilst you might be tempted into believing that you are somehow doing a tenant a favour by renting him a property for 'only £X' (please insert your own expectations), no matter how small a sum this may seem to you it is likely to represent a significant proportion of his disposable income. It is often stated that it costs more to rent than buy a property and in monthly outgoings terms this is quite true. To put this in perspective, the generally accepted minimum salary required to become a tenant is 2½ times its annual rent. After utility bills and council tax, your average tenant is not left with much disposable income.

The tenant is your *customer* so you need to engender 'customer loyalty' by treating him well. If you do this he is far more likely to stay. The days of being able to provide sub-standard homes with poor insulation, inefficient heating and dated bathrooms, kitchens and décor are long gone. Where a landlord skimps in the belief that he will get higher margins, he exposes himself to the risks associated with longer void periods and lower quality tenants. It's also worth mentioning that legislation nowadays (see especially *Chapter 22*) is such that a tenant may report a landlord to the local authority and rogue landlords may be served with improvement notices, fined, or might even be banned from the industry. Whenever possible, you should be aiming for Mr Blue-Chip (*Chapter 9*) since he is far more likely to be able to afford the rent, pay it on time and look after your property.

Furnished or Unfurnished?

The market generally decides what is best in this regard and it's difficult here to say what will be true everywhere or in all situations. That said, some advice will always be valid. First, is the property already furnished and will removing furniture cause you expense and inconvenience? If you are in a similar position to my wife and I were when we let our existing home in 1992, then remove everything that is intrinsically valuable, plus personal items, and leave everything else. You should be prepared, however, for tenants to ask you to make changes and substitutions or remove the occasional piece of furniture. Such requests can become a 'nightmare' to deal with and the longer the property is let the more tenants you'll have and the greater the number of such requests.

If leaving or installing beds, make sure that you provide mattress protectors (to keep tenants happy and the beds clean throughout the tenancy) and be willing to throw away mattresses when you return (for your own sanity). Think carefully about leaving linen and other items which you'll one day need to use again yourself. I'd urge you anyway to consider investigating the costs associated with storage. There are more facilities available today than there were in 1992 when I had this dilemma. If I were to be in that position again, knowing what I now know, I would let unfurnished. The larger the property, the more likely you are to attract tenants with their own furniture. This means that one or other of you will be obliged to store furniture (or the tenants will look elsewhere). Sometimes, leaving furniture in a property can't be avoided, or the storage of bigger items becomes problematic. Under these circumstances, letting with the larger pieces only might be a solution. But I would still urge you not to do this if you can avoid it.

A landlord's repairing obligations do not cover much that you will leave behind, indeed, even in an unfurnished property (where white goods are often the only thing left), a landlord is not *obliged* to repair or replace, and a good tenancy agreement will point this out. That said, here there is an example of a tenant's 'fair expectations'. If you leave something behind, a tenant has an expectation that you'll *take responsibility* for its repair or replacement. Obviously, you would accept to maintain a built-in cooker but, and unless it is specifically stated to the contrary, a tenant will expect maintenance of a free-standing fridge-freezer or washing machine. Simply put, the more you leave behind the greater the tenant's expectations. Bed? Wardrobe? Settee? You left it, he's paid rent for it, he'll expect you to repair or replace it, assuming he hasn't caused the damage to it.

There are types of tenants and the properties they are attracted to when furniture is more of an issue. Those on overseas secondment (*Chapter 9*) may have arrived with just a suitcase and will want every bit of furniture. We have regular and interesting differences of opinion about precisely what should be left for different tenants. Maybe, with a studio, you could leave furniture, after all, it is likely to be let to a 'week-dayer' (*Chapter 9*) who has his own furniture back at home. That said, he might also have an estate car and the wherewithal to bring down spare bits and pieces to part-furnish his pied-a-terre. Whilst there is an argument for furnishing a one-bed flat for first-timers with no furniture, in my experience they usually get by without you doing this. Family and friends often help them out, or they enjoy trips to Ikea.

One thing to bear in mind is that you don't necessarily get that much more in rent, if at all, by letting furnished. So, you're taking that much more risk for no extra financial gain and quite possibly petty arguments arising over whether you'll swap the leather sofa for a fabric one, or the white wardrobe for a plain wooden one. We manage around 90 properties in a large development in the centre of town and, ironically, I have the converse argument with some investors there. By not furnishing, they don't get quite as much in rent, yet their apartments aren't as popular. If three or four are vacant, all else being equal it is usually the unfurnished ones which let more slowly.

Where you do have a reason to furnish your letting, my advice is not to buy the cheapest furniture but some that will last. The block where we manage 90 apartments was completed in around 2004 and landlords were encouraged in those days to furnish with every conceivable item. The ones who saved money buying cheap furniture have purchased replacements, sometimes many times over. Those who bought more expensive but better things are sometimes still using the original furniture. But please don't waste your money on toasters, kettles, microwaves, or similar items. Provide the bare essentials in that regard.

Décor

Most of the time, a tenant has several properties to choose from and décor undoubtedly plays a major part in his decision-making. In an ideal world, your property will be left in a fresh condition. It will have had a recent lick of paint and be as inoffensive in decorative terms as possible. The days of everything having to be magnolia are probably gone, but it is still safe to say that the property ought to be presented in as neutral a colour scheme as possible. Whites, light-greys, and pastel colours are all fine, but bear in mind that someone will have to touch up the paintwork periodically, so keep it to as few colours as possible and make sure you have a note of what the exact paints/shades/makes are.

Whilst paints don't keep forever and that on the walls will fade over time, if you have spare paint left over it's a good idea to leave it at the property for touch-up jobs. But don't fill the only available storage space with part-filled tins, left over wallpaper, spare tiles, bits of carpet or scraps of vinyl. Tenants need somewhere to store their own belongings and you'll find your old paint thrown away if you take up an inordinate amount of room.

Sometimes a feature wall is acceptable, but by and large I would suggest that all such walls are painted over. Remember my blue bathroom that was repainted? The landlord who ended-up with a Bristol Rovers fan as a tenant could as easily have had an application from a Bristol City supporter when blue wouldn't have been acceptable! Wherever wallpaper is left, it causes problems sooner or later. I had a landlord with a former show home which had wallpaper on the staircase. Inevitably it got damaged. He was prudent in that he'd kept a roll or two for such eventualities, but nonetheless it would have been far easier to rectify a few knocks to paintwork.

Whilst it's faster and easier to coat woodwork with eggshell, the finish is nowhere near as durable. Our shop and offices were refurbished to someone else's specifications using eggshell and within a short period of simple use (as opposed to abuse) it needed to be done again. Keep woodwork simple and paint in a white gloss. We have several modern apartments where grey woodwork looks okay, but try and avoid alienating potential tenants with colour schemes which are overbearing. Similarly, keep ceilings simple and use a white emulsion. Wipeable paints are a good idea, especially in kitchens and bathrooms. In these rooms, you can stray from the whites and magnolias, but keep it neutral.

There was a time when properties were fitted with wooden interior doors and, in some, they can look very smart indeed. We look after a tenancy in an ex-local authority three-bed semi where new woodwork has been fitted throughout and the doors are expensive and good-looking. They were fitted before the owner decided to let the property and I'm certain that, were he to have known, he wouldn't have spent so much on them. Nonetheless, this is an example of where the trouble and expense he went to led to a feature which has proved popular with applicants. The colour of these doors is such that they don't make the hallways look dark or uninviting. Yet there are examples of properties I can think of fitted with dark wooden doors which make these places look gloomy and off putting. This is particularly true of smaller rooms and hallways. My suspicion is that by staining or varnishing doors it was somehow cheaper. They might have looked okay in the 1980s when the property was brand new, but they absolutely don't look as good as white doors now they are older, marked and showing signs of wear and tear. Invariably, white is the answer.

Floor Covering

An accidental landlord might not wish to make any changes to flooring given his circumstances and I fully understand this, but anyone else really does need to give floor coverings consideration.

Bathroom and kitchen floors

I deal more fully with bathrooms and kitchens later in this chapter but it is convenient to discuss their floors here. For my money, a vinyl of some description is the best option. For hygiene reasons it's also better in en-suites and cloakrooms. At home, I prefer to have warm feet in the winter, and we've fitted carpets in upstairs bathrooms, but our home isn't going to have a continual stream of different occupants using it. No matter what your personal preference, vinyl in bathrooms is usually the way forward when letting. And if you're an accidental landlord, you might want to think about the prospect of moving back into your home after a few years when all manner of strangers have been using your nicely carpeted bathrooms.

You might have ceramic tiles in your kitchen. If so, you won't want to bother with unnecessarily covering them up. But a dropped saucepan may well chip a tile, so if you have the chance to specify something for the future I would avoid ceramic tiles. We recently had a new kitchen fitted at home. The cupboard carcasses were smaller than the originals, so we needed to change the flooring. It was originally ceramic tiles, and we were unable to find identical ones anywhere. The solution was to lay a self-levelling latex screed over the tiles and place vinyl on top. I mention this in case you were to believe that changing the tiles would have involved the grief of lifting them all. You cannot simply lay vinyl over tiling as the joints will show through. Sometimes, hardboard is used as a base, but this obviously cannot be securely and easily fixed to tiling. We manage a lovely three-bed property with expensive, high-gloss ceramic tiles which are about 750 mm square. The kitchen looks fabulous, but the owner has admitted that he wouldn't have laid that flooring had he known he was going to let out the place. He does have a few spare tiles and I'm sure that someone, somewhere, will be prepared to replace one or two if necessary. But at what cost?

If a tenant does damage something, there is the deposit (*Chapter 21*) from which to make deductions if arranging repairs or replacement, but the larger the sums involved the less likely the tenant will be willing to agree to this without the two of you needing to go to arbitration. Vinyl, by comparison, might show signs of the dropped pan, but it is unlikely that it will have to be replaced and if that were needed the expense is likely to be much less. When selecting vinyl floor covering, consider closely the quality of the vinyl and standard to which it is fitted. A cheap vinyl badly laid will not stand the rigours it will inevitably be subjected to. Apart from anything else, the white goods will inevitably need to be moved regularly and no matter how much care is taken when lifting washing machines and freezers the flooring is at risk. The cheaper, more lightweight the flooring, the more likely it will be to suffer from tears and abrasions. The fitting is important and it's always an idea to let the fitter know that the property is to be let. If he's any good, he'll have useful tricks to employ in such properties.

At the extreme upper end of the scale are expensive vinyls manufactured by companies such as Amtico and Karndean. These are not fitted in rolls, which tend to be secured just at the edges. They are supplied as individual tiles or in narrow strips which are each securely fixed. They are fitted by specialists and, whilst expensive, are incredibly durable and will take a lot more punishment than other forms of vinyl. They come in realistic imitations of wood flooring, marble and other materials; the sort of high-end product which will prove attractive to would-be tenants. This vinyl is laid on a latex screed to ensure a great finish.

Somewhere between the cheap, DIY roll from your local hardware super-store and top of the range flooring which might involve a second mortgage, is something that will be adequate. In apartments, laminates do occasionally get used in these areas but are susceptible to water spillages of one sort or another and most don't react well, especially if the spillage is not wiped-up quickly and completely.

Living rooms and hallways

I have an almost automatic hate of laminate flooring in downstairs or main living areas. This is because, all too often, I see it fitted as an afterthought and cheaply. It's usually necessary to use small mouldings at the edges to hide them. In large rooms, it might be argued that this isn't too big a deal. Around door frames, however, it is practically impossible to successfully follow the shape of the architrave and there are often lots of tiny lengths of moulding and joins.

This looks messy from the start, but once a vacuum cleaner has knocked into mouldings they inevitably come loose, and their appearance deteriorates from there onwards. And they are a perfect haven for dust and debris. If laminate is fitted correctly, in my opinion, the skirting boards and door frames/architraves need to be removed and, once re-fitted, they will cover the edges far more successfully.

Although I am not a great fan of laminate, at home we recently had engineered wood flooring replaced with it. Because there was already well laid flooring in place, the fitter was able to install the laminate under the skirting and architraves. It might be worth speaking to a fitter if you find yourself in this position. If you go to the trouble and expense of doing this properly, you are far less likely to have ongoing problems than you will with carpet. But please avoid the temptation to fit cheap laminate flooring. This has a habit of showing chips and tears around joins and can quickly make a room look scruffy. Whilst I don't suggest spending huge sums on carpet, I'm not sure that you can ever spend too much on well-fitted laminates. They can last much longer than carpets, suffer far less damage and can be cleaned and brought back to looking as good as new without too much effort.

Engineered real wood flooring, parquet flooring and the like are expensive alternatives. If they are already fitted, then that's fine, but the likelihood of ongoing maintenance (oiling, varnishing, sanding to get rid of gouges, etc.) makes them a troublesome choice and to be avoided. A good laminate is far more durable and requires virtually no maintenance. If you don't wish to go to the trouble and expense of laminate flooring fitted correctly, then carpets can be successful. Consider a Berber twist instead of a cut pile and go for something which has more synthetic content than you might for your own home. Avoid the temptation to specify too pale a colour, certainly the carpets used in most show homes and new properties tend to be too light. I usually suggest something with specks of different colours, rather than a plain carpet as I find that the slight pattern hides a multitude of minor sins. Don't forget the underlay. If you buy cheap underlay, it won't last as long as a better quality one. And, even when new, it won't make the carpet feel soft and inviting. A good quality underlay will give the impression that the carpet is a lot more expensive than it was.

At all costs, avoid heavily patterned carpets of which your grandparents would have been proud. You have no idea what sort of furniture your tenants have. By making them neutral, a tenant won't dismiss your property over a clash of colours or styles. Being too contemporary might have a similar effect on a tenant's desire to rent your property. Most of us are quite conservative in our tastes. The one area where carpets tend to show signs of wear and tear first is in doorways. A tip that I've picked up from carpet fitters is to consider having two rows of carpet gripper either side of the door-bar. These high traffic areas often show signs of fraying, and this simple trick can help reduce the stress at the edge of the carpet. It will take the fitter literally seconds longer to fit these extra lengths of gripper and cost only an 'extra few pence'.

There is a landlord locally with whom we now refuse to deal. In part this is down to his treatment of a tenant's deposit. He regards it as the means to bring his properties up to scratch, but he chooses to ignore fair wear and tear. This stance causes disputes with vacating tenants. Specifically, he has a strange approach to carpets, which is worth bringing to your attention as one to avoid. He has bought acres of cheap, thin and not hard-wearing carpet which he keeps in store. He fits every property with brand new carpet from this stock at each change of tenant. The problem is that no matter how short-lived the tenancy the carpets do all need changing every time a tenant departs. Simply because whenever the tenant drags a chair from under the dining-table, or moves a settee, or pushes a vacuum cleaner around, marks are left on the carpet which cannot be removed.

We had one tenant who thought he was doing the right thing by having the carpet professionally cleaned and it practically fell apart. This tale illustrates the folly of buying cheap. But don't go to silly extremes and spend too much. Carpet has a lifespan which will be brought up in the event of a dispute over damages, and rarely is expensive carpet worth fitting. A mid-price carpet ought to be perfectly adequate. Most carpet salesmen and fitters are aware of the sort of carpet that will be appropriate for rented accommodation and it's worth soliciting their opinion. A good agent also ought to be able to provide some input.

Repairs to laminates

Little can usually be done about damage to vinyl, but there are specialist companies that are able to repair laminates. This doesn't mean that you will get away with cheap laminates, it simply means that there is a solution which might prove to be of use if you do suffer with damage to your laminate flooring.

Bedroom carpets

A significant number of tenants from overseas just don't get the British fixation with carpets and would rather see hard flooring in every room. If I'm honest, in houses I hate laminate in bedrooms full-stop. I don't care how well it's fitted or what type it is. And I have yet to see a laminate fitted in an upstairs room which seems right. That said, in apartments where all the accommodation is on the same floor, I think that it does make sense to consider the same flooring throughout the hallways, living rooms, bedrooms and store cupboards. And it is apartments where most overseas tenants at least start their journey in rented accommodation in this country.

Bathrooms

I speak with landlords regularly about fitting out bathrooms. Quality always comes up in conversation. All too often a landlord will have bought a property with a bathroom which is functional but not attractive. I often find myself asking whether it would compare favourably to the landlord's own bathroom at home. I'm not suggesting that it needs to be top of the range, but it shouldn't give reason for someone to say no to renting your property.

The need for a bath and shower

The bathroom needs to have both a shower and a bath. This might be a shower fitted over the bath or in a separate cubicle, but ideally you should offer both in the family bathroom. Whenever we advertise a bathroom with no shower, viewers want a shower. Whenever we advertise with shower and no bath, viewers want a bath. I don't see the point in bucking the trend. Wherever possible, offer tenants both. This is especially important in a home likely to attract families which might have babies, when a bath is crucial. If there is an en-suite shower-room then a family bathroom with just a bath *might* be an acceptable compromise.

Shower screen or curtain?

From a practical point of view, a shower curtain is better than a fitted shower screen. Even the best screens have problems with seals and the inevitable water ingress and potential for damage will exist. But don't go for the cheapest of curtain poles; specify one which is fixed securely to the wall(s). The worst scenario is that the curtain then needs occasional replacement, but these are cheap. A number of hotels that I've stayed in fit a narrow, fixed screen, perhaps 300 mm in width in addition to the curtain. This takes care of the water which runs down the wall and ends up on the floor or behind the bath panel. With just a narrow screen, it's possible to lean around and turn the bath taps on without needing to open the screen. This reduces the likelihood of wear and tear to the seal.

Mains or electric shower?

If you have a combination boiler and, therefore, good water pressure, you can possibly get away with having a tap and shower combination arrangement. If you haven't got a combination boiler and your pressure is anything less than ideal, you'll likely need to consider either a pump which might be positioned under the bath or in an airing cupboard, or else an electric shower. Savvy tenants have been known to test showers at viewings. Seemingly, low pressure in this regard is a common problem in the rental market.

The downside with electric showers is the continual need for maintenance in hard water areas. A build-up of limescale is inevitable and often a replacement shower is the only solution with anything but the most expensive units. Whilst an electric shower need only cost a couple of hundred pounds, it needs fitting and sometimes this will entail pipework alterations and tiling or other decorative considerations. If you are considering a property refurbishment, be sure to include this alongside the heating system. It's easily overlooked, but when dealt with at the outset needn't cause too much grief or expense.

Retro-fitting electric showers

A word to the wise with regards to retro-fitting showers in bathrooms. There was a time when baths were fitted which had lips at the opposite end to the taps. Whether this added style or made the act of laying down in a bath more comfortable, I don't know. What I do know, however, is that it sometimes has unintended consequences when retro-fitting an electric shower. It's sod's law that the most convenient end to fit the shower is the end with the lip. What this means in practice is that, whenever someone showers, water bounces off them and onto the wall beneath the shower head. It then runs downwards and, because the lip prevents it from making its way to the bath, it pools and eventually runs down the bath side onto the floor. This is the cause of some unsightly bath panels and damage to wooden skirting boards; and in the extreme to floorboards beneath the vinyl. Alternatively, it makes its way through the gap in the grouting and sealant, loosening the tiles. Either way, it causes the landlord an entirely unnecessary headache.

Bear in mind also, the position of windows. Sometimes this makes the siting of the shower head challenging. It might also affect the decision regarding the shower curtain pole. What is sometimes suggested as a solution is locating the shower head midway along the bath's length. If this is the chosen solution, beware cheap circular shower curtain poles. They are inevitably a nightmare to keep in position for any length of time and, when using such an arrangement, the curtain tends to get wet and clings to whoever is showering. Far better to have a conventional straight pole running the length of the bath. A more drastic and potentially far more expensive solution is simply to turn the bath around. But this isn't always a practical option and will inevitably involve far more plumbing work.

Tiling

Be sure to have full height tiling around any bath with a shower fitting. Not to do so will result in the tenant showering regardless leading to damaged paintwork and loosened tiling through water running down the walls. Even if at this stage your tenant is happy, he won't be when you argue over deductions from his deposit. We had a spate of tenancies where there was an en-suite shower but only a bath with a shower attachment in the family bathroom. The attachment was installed to enable children's hair to be washed or possibly for an adult to lean over when washing their hair without the need for a proper bath or shower. Tiling stopped maybe five or six courses above the lip of the bath. Despite this being entirely obvious and it being pointed out to viewers, we had several instances where a tenant or his visitor decided to shower in the bath. Since the walls weren't fully tiled there was consequent damage to the walls. As an aside, bath panels are often damaged if a tenant leans over in this manner.

Some older bathrooms have tiles embossed with images, e.g. of ships, windmills or flowers at random. I don't know exactly when these were fashionable or for how long the fashion lasted, but I guarantee that nobody is now building new properties with tiles of such 'dubious' taste. Please keep tiles white or contemporary. I'm not a fashionista, but doubtless Googling tile retailers will bring to your attention myriad acceptable styles. Make sure that the grouting and sealant is clean. Dirty grouting is unsightly and unhygienic. More to the point, it may lead a tenant to think you have condensation mould issues (*Chapter 14*). There are readily available products which make the removal of sealant quite easy. Please don't try and do it without the aid of such a product. It will take you a lifetime of scraping with a sharp knife and you are unlikely to make a good job of it.

Re-applying silicon seal

Having removed the old silicon from, say, a bath please engage the services of someone who knows how to apply new sealant and is proficient at it. All your hard work will be undone if the bath or shower isn't sealed properly. If you do intend to do it yourself, make sure that the bath is completely full of water and the area to be treated completely dry. Apply a uniform size bead in a continual run the entire length of the gap, so that it overlaps slightly with the tiles and the bath. Tidy it up if necessary. A tradesman will use his damp finger to do this, although it doesn't taste particularly nice and I'm sure there are warnings on the container suggesting that this is not a good idea. Then leave it for at least 24 hours with the water in the bath.

By doing it this way, the sealant will fill the biggest gap with which it will need to contend. Doing it with the bath empty means that when it is filled with water the seal is immediately put under stress and is likely to fail quite quickly. One thing that is sometimes overlooked is the reason for the grouting and sealant being there is the first place. Making the area look nice cosmetically is only part of the story. They are both there to prevent water from getting beneath the tiling and behind the bath or shower. Water will loosen tiles and destroy plasterboard. It will also damage plaster and brickwork. In time it will rot timbers, floorboards, joists, bath and shower cubicle supports, etc. And, just for good measure, it has a habit of running downhill and if from upstairs destroys the aesthetics of ceilings and walls downstairs in your living room or kitchen. Or in your neighbour's apartment.

We have replaced several shower cubicles in a development of apartments built a few years ago. Neglect allowed water ingress and entire cubicles needed replacing. This also involved the replacement of the studwork behind, together with the plasterboard and tiling. A few pounds spent following proactive and regular inspections would have saved what ended up costing nearly £2,000 a time to rectify.

Heated towel rails or radiators?

Clearly there will be wet towels after a bath or shower. Your tenant will need somewhere to dry these and (with apartments in particular) a heated towel rail is an absolute must. Even in a house with a garden and washing line, a sensible towel rail is preferable. Who amongst us doesn't like a warm towel following a leisurely bath?

Extractor fans

This is an area of contention with tenants and landlords. A good property will have an extractor fan in the bathroom but often there is an isolator switch in the hallway, above the bathroom door. On inspections, my staff ensure that these switches are turned on and note this on their visit report. This is because an awful lot of tenants simply turn them off. They do this because the fan keeps them awake at night and, if someone gets up in the middle of the night, they can't get back to sleep. Even if you have a window, you really ought to have a fan. But try and organize it so that it can't be isolated, or so that it comes on with humidity, or movement. That way, even if the window isn't opened, the room will still benefit from ventilation thereby reducing the risk of condensation mould (*Chapter 14*).

Bathroom suites

Rather like Henry Ford and his black Model T Ford, I suggest that you have any colour you like, so long as it's white. You don't have to have a contemporary style, just make sure you don't have a seashell shaped suite or something else that is likely to be of limited appeal. Free-standing baths and fancy contemporary shower cubicles are fine, but don't go off at a tangent which only like-minded individuals will appreciate. Try to appeal to the masses.

Repairs to bathroom suites

Sometimes you'll come across a bath or basin which has been damaged. Often this has been caused by something being dropped on it. The difficulty with this sort of damage is that an insurance claim often won't cover the cost of the whole suite and a replacement won't necessarily match those items not covered. I frequently come across slightly mis-matched bathroom suites for, I suspect, exactly this reason. I have also witnessed DIY repairs to suites with far from satisfactory results. There are, however, a growing number of companies who offer 'invisible repairs' to bathroom suites. The success or otherwise of any repair will depend upon the exact nature of the damage, but I've found on several occasions that sending the company a photograph of the damaged area brought in a competitive quote.

Lighting

It's possible that your property was built at a time when an open bayonet fitting to the ceiling was quite acceptable. This is no longer so. If you are in any doubt about electrics in the bathroom, check out the regulations, but preferably speak to a qualified electrical contractor. The issue is likely to arise anyway when you seek to obtain your electrical inspection condition report (EICR) (*Chapter 15*). Specifically, with the bathroom light, I would suggest an enclosed fitting with a long-lasting LED lamp inside it.

Other bathroom electrics

We had a property a few years ago in which the landlord had previously lived. It was a large room and a washing machine had been installed. He might have been content with the risks for his family, but this sort of thing is absolutely at odds with the creation of a safe environment for your tenant. We had another where the airing cupboard was situated in the bathroom which had a double socket for white goods. Those goods presented a danger in themselves, but the sockets added a further level of risk in that a tenant could plug in a hairdryer, radio or other appliance which might then have been balanced on the edge of the bath. Water and electricity are not good when inappropriately mixed and special care should be taken with electricity in bathrooms (and kitchens: below). An ingress protection (IP) regulation search will also throw up details regarding the siting of other electrics.

Kitchens

Like the bathroom, the kitchen needs to be taken seriously. There isn't necessarily a formula, but it needs to be both presentable and functional. Its exact nature will depend upon the size of the home and the likely number of occupants, so give this some thought. It is clear to me that builders do not always take as much care over this as they should.

Storage

Tenants may well have more cake-tins and kitchen gadgets than you do. That you might regard the need for certain things as 'crazy' is neither here nor there. I have already alluded to an improvement in standards generally, but this isn't always the case. I mentioned earlier in this book a development of 200+ apartments which were released to the market. This is a development where kitchens were either not fully understood by the developers or simply treated with disdain. Either way, they got it badly wrong. Whereas the apartments should have easily achieved better rents than older competitors, the kitchens were one reason why they didn't. Predominantly this development was made up of one-bed apartments. Maybe the designers assumed that all were to be occupied by single people and maybe that they would always eat out. Whatever their justification, the kitchens were woefully inadequate. They came with only one wall cabinet and shelf plus two under-counter cupboards. A tenant might store food, the means to cook it, or the means to eat it. There simply wasn't space for all three. So, woe betide any tenant who dares to be adventurous and who needs space for anything that he isn't prepared to store on a work surface. And I sincerely hope there won't be too much, since having used it for his coffee machine, toaster, juicer, food mixer, kettle etc., he'll have precious little room for anything else.

I know of a well-appointed studio which achieves more rent than it ought. Part of this is due to the appointment of the kitchen. And this will always be the case. Get it right and you'll benefit. Get it wrong and you'll get less rent than you ought, and your property will take a lot longer to let.

Whether or not you provide white goods is a choice for you. If you do, make sure that the fridge-freezer has a large freezer compartment. Ice boxes no longer cut it with tenants. If you don't provide one, ensure that there is adequate space for one. If for whatever reason, it must go under the counter, try to ensure that there is space there for a fridge and a separate freezer. If the boiler must go in the kitchen and it ends up in a cupboard, make sure that there are plenty of other cupboards available for storage. If the extractor hood is integral and looks like a cupboard, ensure that there are others alongside it.

Quality and style

The actual quality and style of the kitchen might not be the same as you would provide for yourself, but it ought to be up to the job. To be fair, most kitchens from builders' merchants and DIY stores nowadays are suitable. The kitchen is a room which will not only be used by your tenant but also be seen by his guests. I think that it's perfectly understandable for someone to turn his nose up at a kitchen which is out-dated, well-worn, or defective in some way. Most of us want to think that our friends and colleagues consider we lead a comfortable lifestyle. Nowadays, the most popular kitchens have modern, clean lines. The wooden doors with quaint brass dangling handles might be right up your own street and were once popular. There will be tenants for whom this is also ideal, but the majority will want something more contemporary.

Designing your kitchen

Beware when designing your kitchen of using doors and drawer fronts which have a plastic laminate covering. Heat from ovens, grills and toasters can damage these quite easily and deducting from a tenant's deposit for something which is inevitable because of design may prove tricky. You can cover some of the risk by highlighting in a tenancy agreement that modern grills are designed to be used with the door shut, or that care should be exercised when using a toaster directly underneath a unit, but prevention through design is far better than through instruction or enforced repair. If you are re-fitting a kitchen, remember that white goods need to have moulded plugs and so there ought to be adequate sockets under the counter. You can no longer simply drill a hole and fit a new plug. Bear in mind also that there are companies offering discounted refurbishment of kitchens, achieved by simply replacing door and drawer fronts and worktops, leaving the original carcasses in place.

Tiling

The herb is to the kitchen tile what the sailing ship is to the bathroom tile. Once upon a time it was arguably fashionable, but nowadays the attraction is questionable. Whereas white or contemporary is the flavour of the bathroom tile, the kitchen does allow for rather more flexibility. Once again, if in doubt, check out with tiling retailers and look at what they are promoting. Or, as I suggested in earlier chapters, look at properties being offered elsewhere. Show homes are a good source of inspiration and you'll also be able to witness my criticism of the lack of storage now provided in some new properties.

Splashbacks

Kitchen sink splashbacks are often overlooked, especially in new-build properties. No doubt it is cheaper to construct a house with only a small or no splashback. Even were you to live in a property lacking splashbacks yourself, you would encounter problems. Grease and general grime from cooking and washing-up will make short work of destroying paintwork. Stainless steel or tiles behind the hob and tiles around the sink and on sills is the obvious answer for a quiet maintenance-free life. There are nowadays several attractive, often bespoke, glass equivalents, but they can be expensive.

Electrics

If you are re-fitting a kitchen, this is the ideal opportunity to right this issue. Look at your own kitchen. Do you have adequate sockets? Would it be sensible to provide more? A tenant will likely have a fridge-freezer, a washing machine, maybe a dishwasher and a tumble-dryer. I bet they'll have a toaster, a kettle, and a microwave. What about a juicer, or a coffee machine? A food mixer, a computer? The list goes on. Please don't assume that you're buying a property that will be fully compliant. We recently came upon an example where sockets were sited too close to the hob. This only came to light when the hob was being changed and the fitter refused to do this because of the sockets. Once again, electrical regulations should be (and are easily) investigated. If you are in any doubt, be sure to consult a qualified electrician and again your EICR inspection is highly relevant.

Lighting

Give serious consideration to changing those multi-light fittings in a kitchen which are a haven for dust and grime, and which are forever getting damaged through their frailty. Why not go the whole hog and install recessed LED spotlights? With a long lifespan, these really are becoming features with benefits appreciated by tenants. And they are comparatively cheap when compared with ugly and unreliable alternatives. Under cupboard lighting is something that I personally am quite ambivalent about. Having established that I am not a designer, the aesthetics argument won't necessarily swing me. But, if you don't have them, then you have one thing less to go wrong and one set of lamps less to argue about with the tenant when he leaves.

Worktops

If you already have an expensive granite worktop, then there's not much that you can do about this. But, if you haven't, then I would suggest that you don't go out and specify one for your new kitchen. Get the worktop professionally fitted. A properly mitred join is nowadays strong and effective and looks far better than the DIY aluminium joining strips of yesteryear. Avoid the high gloss black, or indeed other coloured high gloss finish. A tenant will never take as much care as you with your property and these will show marks more quickly than others. The colour will naturally depend upon units and tiling.

If you can, have a hand in its design and think about things such as the position of the joints in relation to the sink and draining board. Modern joints are much better nowadays, but even they won't take kindly to continual immersion in washing-up water. If you have a perfectly serviceable worktop which has suffered from damage, check out 'kitchen worktop repairs' or similar and you'll come across several companies that may well be able to effect a repair, saving you the time and money involved with worktop replacement.

Ovens and hobs

In my experience, tenants prefer built in cookers with a gas hob and an electric oven. From a maintenance perspective, a built-in gas hob won't have a lid that can cause issues and you won't have the small gap between the cooker and the units which are a nightmare to clean without dragging the cooker out of position. The choice of hobs nowadays is enormous, but I would take a sensible approach. So long as it has four burners and is easily cleaned, it's probably adequate. Try and avoid things which will cause problems. You might already have an induction hob in place and if that's the case then this is something which can be dealt with; tenants can be educated. If you don't, then don't decide to fit this sort of thing. You're just creating potential problems further down the line.

Washing Machines

With legislative issues being what they are, I personally cannot get too concerned whether a landlord wishes to provide a washing machine or not. Although currently, most landlords of unfurnished properties do provide them, and some tenants won't have their own. If you lack a washing machine, don't rush out and buy one, although it might be prudent to be prepared to do so if necessary. If the property does not have easy access to a garden, then your tenants are likely to wish to dry clothes inside. To save no end of potential problems, I would, therefore, suggest a separate tumble-dryer. Not all properties have the space for this, so as a compromise I would consider a combined washer-dryer. A washing machine engineer of any worth will tell you that these are not as effective and that they are just that, a compromise to consider. Please make sure to read *Chapter 14* on Condensation Mould to help understand the risks associated with moisture in properties.

Additional Sockets

The 1960s and 1970s homes to which I so enthusiastically refer elsewhere are defined by one thing other than their age; the paucity of electrical sockets provided when built. In the 1960s, we didn't have TVs in every room. We didn't have video recorders, let alone DVD players. We didn't have computers or mobile phones to charge. We didn't have games consoles. We might have had a food mixer, but we certainly didn't have coffee makers, juicers, and toasted sandwich makers. Basically, sockets were provided for a TV, standard lamp, bedside lights (possibly) and maybe two or three kitchen gadgets. When a property is empty, a lack of sockets is more apparent.

If you get an opportunity to do so, get as many additional sockets in as possible. The alternative is that tenants are tempted to use adaptors and extension leads and plug no end of things into the same one. Potentially, this is a disaster waiting to happen.

Consider how these sockets are going to be installed. Try and avoid the necessity for trunking running along skirting boards. Have floorboards lifted where possible and chase into walls if the budget allows. Remember, your property isn't being marketed in isolation and, over time, trunking (covered cabling that stands out from a wall) looks worse than it does when newly fitted (which though cheaper is not attractive to begin with). Would you personally like lots of trunking on your walls? It's a good idea to include sockets here and there that have USB ports for charging phones, etc. Kitchens are favourite for this, and tenants really appreciate these little touches. This is true of any property, no matter how many sockets it may have.

Lighting

Currently too many homes need an incredible variety of different lamps for light fittings. Incandescent lighting is on its way out and has been for several years, but the variety of alternatives is overwhelming. Some of the original low energy lamps (often supplied free by power companies) were virtually useless but, of late, a variety of low voltage or halogen lamp fittings have been introduced. It's becoming clear, however, that LED is beginning to win the war of the lamps.

To make life easier for tenants and especially those from overseas, I advocate a streamlining of lighting types and I believe LED to be worthy of consideration. These lamps last for tens of thousands of hours, and this makes the initial outlay worthwhile. A tenant is responsible for replacing lamps as they fail, but if they don't, then you will need to deal with this and take the cost from a tenant's deposit. Some lamps are becoming quite difficult to source, so trying to ensure that they are all the same will make your life easier as well.

Curtains and Blinds

In my experience it is better to have any curtain poles or blinds fitted to battens which are painted in the same emulsion as the walls. Especially where walls are dry lined, the provision of battens will help to prevent the weight of the curtains and poles dragging the fixings from them and creating unnecessary damage to decorations. And an average tenant may not be quite so gentle as you would in your own home.

If you provide curtains, try and ensure that they are lined and relatively neutral. Rather like the carpets, you want to aim to have them not cause a mismatch with the tenant's own furnishings. You might find that a tenant will pack them away in a bin liner in the airing cupboard and use his own, but curtains will be expected, even in an unfurnished property. That said, the first time you let a property, you might get away without providing them so don't rush out and buy them just yet. But it's best to be prepared to do so. There are any number of shops selling curtains which are of a sufficiently good quality and yet not overpriced. You are unlikely to need to worry about net curtains nowadays.

I'm not a huge fan of blinds for a few reasons. They become untidy quite easily and the mechanisms have a habit of malfunctioning. If you do intend to provide Venetian blinds, then ensure that they have been cut to length, so that there isn't an unsightly and heavy excess of slats at the bottom. This is a lot easier to do than it sounds. There is legislation surrounding blinds,[1] which is another reason I dislike them. It's something else which needs to be managed. In short, cords need to be trimmed to the right length, which makes perfect sense, but they also need 'cleats' (small fixings around which the cords can be wound to hold the blind open or closed and keep the cords out of harm's way). In addition, they need a device which enables the cord to snap apart easily, rather like the little fitting you see sometimes on plugs for sinks. These rules are designed to ensure that children in particular are unable to come to harm.

The only rooms where I personally haven't got a problem with roller blinds are bathrooms and kitchens. Kitchens blinds are troublesome being grease accumulators, so a cheap and cheerful roller blind is preferable to expensive curtains which will require continual cleaning, or Venetian blinds that are a

---

1. See www.rospa.com/campaigns-fundraising/current/blind-cord

problem to clean effectively. If you accept up front that you might need to pay to replace a cheap roller blind periodically, you'll save yourself stress when you realise that your tenant has handed back a dirty and greasy kitchen blind.

Television

I have more unnecessary heated debates over TV reception than I should. And, if you approach things in the wrong way, you'll also have arguments over this. Where a tenant views a property and sees a TV aerial socket, he'll naturally expect that it works. This will mean an aerial in or on the roof, or the wall or balcony of a flat. If, for whatever reason, the socket doesn't work and you aren't prepared to arrange for its repair, then remove it or make it abundantly clear that it is not included. Or risk unhappy tenants.

This never seemed to be a problem in the days of analogue television, and it seems that it is the increased costs of digital aerials that has caused some reticence on the part of landlords. This is simply crazy when you consider the relatively minor costs associated with it. It's a one-off expense which will solve a problem and invariably give no further problems for years. Sod's law states, however, if it's working it may never get used. Some tenants will want Sky, Virgin or similar instead. Saying no to a professionally installed Sky system or cable installation will cause arguments with your tenant. You might find that successive tenants all want different providers, but it would be prudent to allow all of them. Even when Europeans want to install a slightly larger dish it would also be wise to agree.

Once Sky has been installed, it's quite usual for the dish to remain, so you shouldn't end up with dozens of fresh installation holes in your walls following its removal. But lay down in writing some basic rules for tenants to adhere to: professional installation, no drilling holes in window frames, proper securing of cabling, and making good if later removed. All perfectly acceptable and enforceable terms.

Heating and Drying

Nowadays with new properties, heating and drying arrangements are frequently governed by the nature of the development when standard facilities are installed across a range of properties.

Gas-fired central heating

Without doubt, the most popular form of heating for tenants is gas-fired, radiator central heating. That's not to say that other forms of heating will prove so unattractive that you won't find tenants, it's just that a tenant invariably prefers this. The less efficient and uneconomic your arrangements, the longer you can expect to wait for a tenant and the less you can expect in rent. In the extreme, it may be that the only tenants you attract are the sort you probably won't want. Given a choice, I would suggest a combination boiler. This provides better water pressure, negating the need for an electric shower. It's also a lot more efficient and a tenant will appreciate the cost-savings.

Airing cupboards

Some tenants would undoubtedly like an airing cupboard, but this will entail having a hot water cylinder and is simply something else which will cost money to replace at some stage. Unvented systems are becoming ever more popular and provide mains pressure water for showers yet still have a hot water tank for airing purposes. In larger properties with more than one bathroom, this might prove to be the most effective solution. They need regular servicing, however, and will work out comparatively more expensive. I've recently bought an apartment with a combination boiler. In the airing cupboard is a small electric heater. To be honest, I've never turned it on and am unlikely ever to do so. It strikes me that it's too easily left on, tucked away out of sight and if there were to be a problem smoke might be the first indicator.

Air-source or ground source heating?

There are relatively few of these systems installed and I haven't yet come across one in a rental property. There are pros and cons for them and with legislation regarding boilers imminently about to change, I suspect that we will begin to see more of them.

Storage heaters

Blocks of flats often don't have gas. Instead, they rely on some form of off-peak electric heating system. Forget the large and ugly storage heaters of yesteryear; full of bricks and which had to be turned on the day before. These are nowadays slim and unobtrusive, and some can be reasonably efficient.

Oil-filled electric heaters

Where a property still has outdated storage heaters, it is well worth looking at alternatives. In addition to the modern equivalent, there are electrically heated oil-filled radiators which are effective.

Gas fires

Gas fires are present in a small percentage of rental properties, but they need regular maintenance and an annual gas safety check. There are contemporary fires available, but the older models (which may still function quite well) will likely prove unattractive to a tenant.

Open fires

Open fires can be potentially both beneficial and a hindrance. If the property is suited to an open fire, then it can be a real centrepiece and a feature which will be appreciated. But an ugly fireplace serves no real purpose other than to be somewhere to stand birthday cards on the mantelpiece. Chimneys also need regular sweeping. It used to be that a landlord could insist through a term of the tenancy agreement, that a chimney be swept at regular intervals and upon vacation by the tenant. Following the tenant fee ban, however, this might prove to be a prohibited charge (i.e. a fee) and therefore, an unenforceable.

It is common for a fireplace to be described as a 'non-working fire, for decorative purposes only' in a tenancy agreement, but the problem with this is that unless you actually block the chimney or somehow make it 'non-working', you run the risk that it will be used regardless. Other agreements may state that open fires are not allowed, or not without the landlord's express approval, thereby allowing him to vet ongoing safety arrangements such as fireguards and to obtain a sweep's inspection certificate which will be essential for insurance purposes. What may seem reasonable with a family unit may seem less so with sharers when no-one in particular is 'in charge of the fire'. Most people however will be concerned for their own safety and that of those around them.

Oil-fired boilers

These aren't particularly popular, although they are sometimes an alternative where mains gas doesn't exist. You're unlikely to go out and buy such a system out of choice and it's more likely to exist in a property you already own in a remote location or are considering for some reason. Maintenance is just as important as with gas-fired systems. At the inventory stage (*Chapter 16*) the accurate reading of the oil tank's contents is sometimes difficult. With the cost of oil, it isn't unusual for several hundred pounds worth of fuel to be in the tank, so determining exactly who has used what and how much someone owes is paramount. Whenever possible, try and get the tank filled before each tenancy so that the outgoing tenant needs simply to re-fill it just before his departure. This will save time and arguments.

Bottled gas

Calor Gas (or similar) in bottles or a tank is occasionally used to fuel gas boilers, cookers, and fires. Bottle sizes vary, but these can be an effective solution. I once ran a business where the premises were heated in this manner. There were two large tanks in the car park which flicked automatically to the other as one became empty. Regular top-ups can be arranged in the same way as is often the case with oil tanks. Gas safety regulations obviously need to be adhered to.

Carbon Monoxide and Smoke Detectors

For some while, it has been a legal requirement for there to be a working smoke detector on each floor of the accommodation at the start of a tenancy. You should ensure that your tenant signs a form at check-in (*Chapter 16*) — acknowledging that this is the case and that the detectors are indeed working. Furthermore, for rooms where there are solid fuel burners (fires, log-burners, Agas, etc.) there must be a working carbon monoxide (CO) detector.

From 1 October 2022 legislation makes it mandatory to have a CO detector. Detectors may be purchased for modest sums and quite often nowadays come with batteries with an up to ten year lifespan. They can also be wired into the mains electric circuit by a qualified electrician.

Windows

Like you, your tenants will wish to have the best windows they can. In the extreme, single glazed units will affect your energy performance certificate (EPC) rating together with the property's appeal. Double-glazing of many types is available. From a maintenance perspective, UPVC is probably going to be the best option. If specifying new windows, get the best that you can afford. It's cheaper to have less openers but be sure to have at least one per window.

When considering tenant safety and especially in upper storey properties don't overlook the arrangements for preventing a window being opened so far that a child might be able to climb out. This is particularly relevant to 'tilt and turn' windows which are often specified to enable easy cleaning. If you have a property with a sealed unit that has condensation on the inside, then the vacuum will have failed. There are specialist companies providing replacement units and you won't have to buy an entire new window. Apart from the fact that the window will not be as thermally efficient, a 'blown' unit looks ugly. Sometimes it's the little things that make the difference between a property being let and having a void period. Make sure that you have window lock keys for each window. Tenants, like you, will need to arrange for insurance and policies insist on windows having locks and being made secure. And, if locked, a tenant must be able to unlock them in the event of an emergency.

The Garden

Where a property is being let together with a garden or access to one there are always significant areas of concern of which the items below are examples.

Ponds
If the property has a pond, give serious consideration to filling it in. This won't always be possible of course, but a pond is a potential liability, especially where

children are concerned. If filling it in isn't an option, how about securely fencing it in? Is it small enough to have a secure grill placed over the top? I saw a property once where the landlord was a Koi keeper. He was reticent to do anything drastic, since the fish were his pets and were quite old and valuable. I keep Koi myself and I understood his position. They have an incredible lifespan and circumstances caught him up in a hurry, leaving him with no alternative but to let his property with the pond and fish in the short-term at least. He was fortunate in finding tenants who were even prepared to feed them for him. Nonetheless, the solution was far from ideal. We had another landlord with what was little more than a wildlife pond, but he steadfastly refused to fill it in. He even tried to insist on the tenants keeping duckweed and blanket-weed under control. Take my advice and don't make problems for either your tenant or yourself.

Greenhouses

These are as popular in British gardens as ponds are. They also present several potential problems, once again often child-related. The greenhouse won't drown a child but falling glass from an ill-maintained one is a potential risk. Malfunctioning sliding doors are a similar cause for concern. And, how upset would you be if a tenant's child allowed a wayward football to crash through the glass?

My suggestion is to remove smaller greenhouses if possible and make sure that, if one is left, it is as safe as possible. And accept that your tenant probably isn't going to be as keen to tend your Fuchsias as you. He may never step inside the greenhouse except when he reluctantly fetches out the lawnmower. When you come back to it, it may be overgrown and even less sturdy than it was when you left. It's only a greenhouse!

Decking

I personally have a pathological hate of decking. But there are acres of it fitted in gardens throughout the land and there is a chance that a property you intend to let out will have at least a small area of decking. Make sure that it is in good repair and that it has been recently pressure-washed and treated with some sort of stain (preferably with a mildew inhibitor). Broken decking, or skating rinks are disasters waiting to happen. If your tenant suffers a broken bone he will have plenty of time to watch adverts on TV that will be tempting him to start a 'no-hay, no-pay' claim. And in the extreme, you don't need a visit from the council.

Patios

These can be like decking in their propensity for problems. Pressure-wash them and deal with wobbly, loose, or uneven slabs prior to the start of a tenancy.

Lawns

When you first let your property, ensure that the lawn has been mowed, and the edges trimmed. Provide your tenants with the means to keep it in the same condition. A cheap electric mower will usually suffice but ensure that you leave an adequate lead with a residual current device (RCD) (safety mechanism) and make sure that there are matching instructions and a user manual. Providing a strimmer is an equally good idea. Or don't be at all surprised to learn that the lawn isn't tended because 'the landlord didn't leave me anything to do it with'. Nine times out of ten, your lawn won't be in the same good condition when the property is returned to you. It's a good idea to accept this from the outset.

Flowerbeds

You might be green-fingered, but there's every chance that your tenant has different views on how to spend his spare time. Your tenancy agreement should make the tenant responsible for keeping weeds down, but don't expect him to properly tend to your plants. He probably won't know the difference between more exotic specimens and your average weed. He almost certainly won't be familiar with the correct manner of pruning and trimming plants. Leave basic hand tools to negate his arguments when he leaves a jungle on his departure.

Hedges

If you have miles of leylandii to block out unsightly views or nosey neighbours, then your tenants are likely to be appreciative of the consequential privacy. They are unlikely, however, to be pleased at the prospect of spending entire weekends twice a year tending them. If you have significant hedges or bushes that need trimming, then arrange for a gardener to deal with this periodically. Instead of the hedge putting off a tenant or becoming unsightly and overgrown, he will see the gardener as a benefit. You can make a tenant responsible for tending modest beech or privet hedges, but you do need to take a sensible approach to anything of any magnitude.

Fences

When fences come down in storms, letting agents' telephones light up like Christmas trees. Entire estates call to report such problems and they invariably take weeks to sort out with all available panels in the country having been bought up by those fortunate enough to have got to the front of the queue. Sometimes, establishing who owns the fence is difficult. Do yourself a favour and establish in advance precisely which fences you are responsible for. You can usually get this information from the title deeds for the property. It's not as simple as it being a joint responsibility with the neighbours, although sometimes it is. Tenants have a habit of getting irritated by becoming at one with their neighbours, especially if it's a neighbour's responsibility and he's reluctant to do anything about it. Whatever the case, in the event of fencing being damaged, communicate with your tenant and try and keep him happy.

Driveway and Garages

This is closely related to parking which I cover in *Chapter 12*. The larger the property, the more likely it is that your tenant will want both. For most of us, the garage doesn't necessarily get used to park a car in. But it is useful storage space and that a tenant doesn't own a property doesn't mean he hasn't collected a lot of belongings. And what is often overlooked by landlords is that there are a growing number of people who are riding expensive motorcycles. My own garage contains an awful lot of belongings which no doubt I could dispose of if I had no garage, but I appreciate it because of my motorcycle. A good sized and secure shed with a wide doorway is sometimes cited as an alternative.

Sometimes, a landlord will let his property without use of the garage. If it is entirely separate, perhaps around the corner in a block, then this isn't necessarily that big a deal. It does cause problems, however, if it's on the property itself. If a landlord stores items in the garage, presumably he wants access to them periodically. How is access arranged? At what intervals and at what time of the day or week? You must remember that it is your tenant's home, and he is entitled to the quiet and peaceful enjoyment of it. This doesn't mean that you shouldn't play the drums on his doorstep on a Sunday morning—although you shouldn't—it means that you've let the property to him, and he is entitled to carry on with his life without constant interference. Also remember that, in law, a tenant has the right to exclude all others from the property, landlord included. Don't forget about my 'happy tenant'. It's also worth pointing out that, in law, unless your tenant has unfettered access to the entire property, then technically it is the landlord who is responsible for the council tax. Is storing your belongings there really that necessary?

Loft Spaces

Not allowing unfettered access here also raises the issue of whether you should be responsible for the council tax. Sometimes a landlord would rather store his own belongings in the loft. In addition to the inconvenience to the tenant there is also the question of security. No inventory clerk will access a loft and, even were they to agree, they would not rifle through boxes and itemise the contents. And whilst it is possible to put a padlock on the loft hatch, access is often required for maintenance.

Occasionally a landlord expresses concern about the prospect of a tenant falling through a ceiling and causing damage. I'm sure that this does happen occasionally, but I personally have only ever known builders to fall through ceilings. I don't recall a single occasion where a homeowner or a tenant did so. In an ideal world, the loft will be fully accessible and have proper floorboards as this would remove such a risk. In truth, most lofts are simply partially boarded, to enable access to water tanks and for the occupant to store his Christmas tree or suitcases. You would be wise to board the loft at least partially and to provide lighting. Similarly, you should provide a fitted ladder for access. You might be happy balancing on a banister and hitching yourself up, but as a landlord you need to do all that you can to provide a safe environment for your tenants. Many service providers, including British Gas, refuse to work on boilers installed in loft spaces where there is no ladder, boarding and light.

Repairing Obligations

Under Section 11(1) of the Landlord and Tenant Act 1985, you are obliged to keep in good repair the structure and the exterior of the property, including drains and external pipes. Furthermore, you are responsible for keeping in good repair any installations for the supply of water, gas, electricity and sanitation, including basins, sinks, baths and sanitary conveniences. You are also responsible for the repair and maintenance of installations for space and water heating.

You have no legal obligation under this legislation for anything over and above this. However, under a variety of other statutory provisions, you have the responsibility to ensure that the property is (in broad terms), 'safe' and 'fit for human habitation': see generally *Chapter 22*, 'The Law of Landlord and Tenant'. A good tenancy agreement ought to draw the tenant's attention to the fact that in law and under the terms of the agreement you have no obligation to repair or replace white goods (fridges, freezers, washing machines, etc.) or other appliances that are supplied at (or after) the start of the tenancy. Regarding the white goods, there are a couple of ways of dealing in advance with anticipated issues. Far better to do so ahead so that the tenant is fully aware up front. If you don't want the cost associated with the repair or replacement of white goods, then inform the tenant immediately they apply to let the property. If they have children and the washing machine is on its last legs, tell them that they are welcome to use it until it breaks down, but that you won't accept responsibility for repairing or replacing it. And have it written into the tenancy agreement.

What you cannot do, however, is seek to pass responsibility for something to the tenants when it comes to safety. You cannot just sell goods to them for a nominal sum and assume that, if they get electrocuted, you're free of all responsibility. You've supplied it and you must take responsibility in this regard.

'Tenant-like manner'

Defined by the courts as long ago as 1953 in *Warren v Keen* (Court of Appeal) this description has been determined to cover the tenant carrying out the sort of minor job which he might fairly be expected to. Changing lamps in light fittings, replacing toilet seats and the like easily fall into this category. As might providing hooks in a cupboard. But 1953 is about as far from 2022 as it is possible to be when it comes to a tenant's likely exposure to jobs about the home. The tenant-like manner argument assumes a degree of competence. I first re-wired a fuse when I was ten or eleven years of age. Under the supervision of my father, it was almost a rite of passage, along with wiring a plug. But many tenants have not benefitted from this type of experience. With moulded plugs, some tenants have never had to change one. And how many appliances do you imagine are out there with an inappropriate fuse, simply because people have little understanding of the need for different fuses for different items?

Were a tenant to install hooks, would he use the correct size drill? Does he even have a drill? How much damage is likely to be caused by overloaded hooks being ripped out of badly drilled holes with inappropriate fixings in a stud-wall or the back of an expensive door?

I once had an irate landlord speak with me concerning a tenant having replaced a £100 Laura Ashley toilet seat with a £30 B&Q version. It seems that the tenant hadn't asked permission to do this. When questioned, it turned out that the original toilet seat had broken, and the tenant simply replaced it. I argued the tenant-like manner approach but was told in no uncertain terms by the landlord that approval ought to have been sought and that it would have been given on a like-for-like basis only. Two things stand out about this tale. The first is that a £100 toilet seat was over the top. It might have been perfect for the owner-occupier but was probably inappropriate in this case in a rented property. The second thing is that I usually find myself having to argue with landlords over replacing items such as this. Even £30 is usually a 'monstrous and unnecessary' expense. I would have loved to see the response of an arbitrator had this gone to dispute.

If it had been a carpet, then I think like-for-like would be fair enough. If the tenant had whipped out a nice kitchen and replaced it with a much cheaper one, then a landlord would have every right to be upset. I do think, however, that things need to be kept in perspective.

Are You Compromising Any of the Issues in *Chapter 13*?

I often tell a prospective landlord he can sometimes get away with a compromise, but the more compromises he expects a tenant to accept, the more likely the tenant is to continue with his search elsewhere. Do you recall that I suggested putting yourself in the tenant's position? Were you his age and in his situation, would you willingly move into a property offered in the condition you are contemplating?

I recently signed up a landlord to a full tenancy management and we advertised his two-bed ground floor maisonette at the top end of market rent for this style of property in the particular area. I told him that we might not be successful, and he was prepared to drop the rent if we didn't find a suitable tenant within the first few days. When he bought it, in my opinion, it required a new kitchen, a new bathroom, complete redecoration, new carpets and the installation of a gas central heating system. I was not involved in the works, but I expect that he wouldn't have had much change out of £12,000.

He elected to do all the work himself with the exception of the bathroom. He has left an almost matching white bathroom suite, added new taps and a new shower with screen, but has left the original tiling. He has, however, had the tiles painted with a new tile-paint which I have not come across before. And, in fairness, it looks a lot better than I thought it would when he described to me what he'd done. In this example, we quickly found a tenant. He accepts that he has a modern, clean, and tidy flat with a fully-functional bathroom. It's not show home condition, but he has gone to some length to ensure that his offering is of a reasonable standard. But imagine the likely reaction of prospective tenants faced with viewing the property in its original condition.

CHAPTER 14

Condensation Mould

You might be wondering why I'm devoting an entire chapter to this subject. Quite simply, it is without doubt the most frequent problem encountered in rental properties. Once you understand the issue, you'll have a far better chance of making the right adjustments to your property or dealing sensibly with your tenant when the issue arises.

Were you to speak to an *average tenant*, then he would report that he's lived in properties where this has been an issue and is caused entirely by factors beyond his control. In his opinion the property is 'damp'. He will suspect rising damp, or penetrative damp, but will be adamant that it has nothing to do with his own lifestyle. Were you to speak with an *average landlord*, then you would hear stories of condensation mould being a problem in his otherwise 'perfect' properties and that it's undoubtedly his tenants' fault. It is quite likely that there is an element of both lifestyle and property maintenance at play whenever condensation mould rears its ugly head.

What is Condensation?

It is important for all parties to fully understand what causes the problem. Once the root cause is understood, you are halfway towards its prevention. Make sure that you do understand and leave your tenant with information. Make it sufficiently detailed, but easy to comprehend. Most councils provide guidance on their websites.

The atmosphere in any room holds water vapour to a greater or lesser extent. The warmer the temperature, the more water vapour the air can hold. When you go on holiday or on the occasional hot day, even in the UK, have you ever noticed that the humidity is high? High humidity is simply a high volume of water vapour in the atmosphere. Water vapour in the air is perfectly natural, as is the fact that when warm air containing water vapour meets a cold surface that vapour will condense. This is the reason why a glass of cold lager will be wet on the outside, and why your bathroom mirror steams up.

The condensing of the water vapour isn't a problem, and neither is the water it leaves behind. It is simply water, harms nobody and rarely affects the surface upon which is has formed. The problems start when nothing is done about that water. When left for a relatively short period of time it is possible for mould to grow. This isn't the place for a biology lesson, but the ensuing mould can be harmful to health, especially that of the young or vulnerable. It starts as tiny black spots, but if left will create swathes of unsightly blackened wall space, paintwork, grouting and sealant. This can be cleaned away using bleach or proprietary mould cleaner and inhibitor, but it is far better to stop it forming in the first place.

There are two types of tenants in particular for whom mould seems to be an issue. Overseas tenants and their guests not used to our winter temperatures who often batten down the hatches and turn up the heating. This starts the cycle in their case. The other is often the relative novice. Possibly the first time he's lived alone or with a partner, he is inexperienced. Maybe his mother used to air the rooms. Maybe it was his parents who paid the heating bills. He's possibly concerned about the magnitude of those bills and the response is to leave windows shut come what may. That said, it may of course be as much of a problem with experienced and wealthy tenants. Whoever they are, they just need a bit of education.

Lifestyle Adjustments

Having established that the air is holding the water vapour, the answer is to change the air. Simply expelling the damp air will prevent the condensation from occurring. Whilst kitchens and bathrooms are invariably fitted with extractor fans and though these are good basic measures, on their own they may well prove to be ineffective. Where a property has been flooded, large dehumidifiers will be used to rid it of the consequential water vapour and help to dry out rooms. In less dramatic circumstances, electric dehumidifiers can work well and one the size of a small suitcase will expel the equivalent of a washing up bowl of water, sometimes twice a day, and for only a few pence in running costs. It's worth noting that the small dehumidifiers which do not use power and instead rely on crystals are virtually a waste of time. It's not that they don't collect water, because they do. It's that they take only a tiny percentage of the vapour from the air and don't come anywhere close to solving the problem. A cupful as opposed to a couple of washing up bowls isn't really scratching the surface. And eight or ten of these scattered around a room is still only eight or ten cupfuls and it makes the room unsightly.

An electric dehumidifier, however, isn't the best solution. The best dehumidifier in the world and by far the cheapest is mother nature. Nowadays, windows are often fitted with trickle vents and using these is better than nothing, but it still isn't particularly effective. The best way of removing moisture from a property is simply to fully open a window on one side of the room/house, together with one on the other side. There is no point in doing this on a damp day, but most of the time it works well. Most people assume that they will be ridding the property of heat and are reluctant to do this. But a couple of minutes last thing before you go to work in the morning and a couple of minutes before retiring to bed will make an incredible difference and a home soon recovers from a relatively small amount of heat loss.

To remove the moisture from the air, it must be in the air and not have condensed and appeared as water on a surface somewhere. The water vapour will only continue to be airborne if the atmosphere is sufficiently warm and therefore heating is as important as ventilation. Neither will work as effectively in isolation. My wife is one of those people who doesn't like the extractor fan being on in the en-suite bathroom since she is a light sleeper and finds it hard to drift off again if someone has been in there at night. We have used the method I've just described since it was explained to us and we can feel the atmosphere change in our tiny en-suite when we open its window wide, together with a bedroom window at the front of the house. It really does work.

In a typical home, the biggest causes of condensation are bathing, showering, cooking, drying clothes and sleeping. We all know about the first three, but most give sleeping no consideration whatsoever. We all expel an enormous volume of water vapour when we breathe. At night, with the windows and curtains drawn, there is nowhere for this to go. Have you ever drawn the curtains in the morning and seen water streaming down the window? When appraising a property, I'm always drawn to window frames, reveals and soffits. These are the areas around the actual window fitting. It's easy to spot those homes where condensation is not wiped away in the mornings. There are an incredible number of tenants who simply get up, get dressed and go to work without even having drawn the curtains. Net curtains, incidentally, don't help with this and often show tell-tale signs of condensation issues by looking grey or even black, especially around the edges. Having said that ventilation is paramount, you need also to consider furniture. Large pieces placed close to a wall, in particular a cold external wall, will often have condensation mould growing behind them. This is because it's impossible to wipe it away each day and it's more difficult to have an effective through draft to change the air behind an obstacle.

After showering or bathing, opening the cubicle door, drawing back the curtain, and wiping down tiles and screens all helps. There are also sprays which can be bought which when applied to tiles and screens encourage the water to run downwards. If the water ends up going down the plug hole it can't cause mould problems. You might think then that if a tenant does everything I've suggested, and there are further things which a tenant can do to help matters, the problem will go away. In a brand-new property built to modern standards this is probably true. In older properties there are many factors to be taken into consideration.

Back to That 1960s House...

I grew up in a house built in 1964. When we moved in, we had 'linoleum' on the floors, single-glazing, and ill-fitting wooden doors. Homes like this were so drafty that it wasn't uncommon for people to have draft excluders on the living room floor, against the crack under the door. You might have seen films or TV shows where there are curtains across doorways which were used when trying 'to keep out the cold'. We were fortunate enough to have an enormous gas boiler in the kitchen and radiators throughout the house. The windows and sometimes internal doorframes were fitted with lengths of foam draft excluder.

And, as if all these potential sources of drafts weren't enough, many houses had open fires which provided ample opportunity for additional ones, as well as a bit of additional heat.

This little trip down memory lane has a purpose. The point is that we might have had water condensation on the windows, but I never remember having condensation mould anywhere. The drafts which existed everywhere, from the skirting board gaps by the edge of the lino to the loft hatch, meant that the air was continually circulating and there was sufficient heat to ensure that condensation was easily dispersed. So, what has happened between the 1960s and now? Quite simply, the nation has gradually become more prosperous, and we have all sought to improve our lot. Literally. Shortly after we moved into this brand new house, my parents installed fitted carpets. The skirting board gap disappeared in one fell swoop. Double-glazing became readily available and affordable. The window gaps disappeared in short order.

In modern times composite front doors have begun to spring up everywhere. Front doors have largely stopped rattling around in the breeze. Open fires have lost their attraction, chimneys have been blocked up, and electric and gas fires have been installed. No more gales down the chimney! Effectively, we began to hermetically seal our homes. Not everyone recognised the risk though. Clothes could be dried on a radiator within a drafty home with less risk, but the habit persisted. Not everyone had a shower in the 1960s or maybe you didn't have a shower every day. Most homes do have a shower nowadays and they generally get used daily. And there are no doubt many other little habits in a modern environment which contribute to condensation problems. Those where these issues persist tend to be the ones where improvements such as those mentioned above have been made to older properties as opposed to newer properties built to a higher standard of insulation. I rarely come across issues in a new property that aren't entirely of the tenant's making.

My Landlord's Flat

Perhaps the best way of describing what contributory factors might lead to condensation mould is to explain this by using a real life example. One of our landlords bought an upstairs maisonette. It was 1960s built and had been a three-bed property which was converted into flats, and he'd bought it from another landlord, with a tenant in situ. The tenant had her daughter and daughter's boyfriend staying there, so there were three adults living in a modestly sized two-bed flat. The number of inhabitants really can have a dramatic effect on condensation. The tenant complained incessantly about the condensation mould, but the original landlord was of the opinion it was down to the tenant's lifestyle. The property had received frequent temporary fixes in the form of redecoration and partial redecoration and the tenant had been advised by the original landlord to buy a dehumidifier.

The landlord, coincidentally, also ran a small lettings agency and, I believe, should have known better. As luck would have it, that tenant left shortly after the property was bought by our landlord. I suggested to the new owner that the problem wasn't necessarily down to his tenant's lifestyle, and I believed that carrying out some work on the property would most likely improve matters and make his life a lot better in terms of ongoing maintenance associated with mould.

The condensation was so bad in this property that water cascaded down the chimney breast and the tiles in the bathroom were permanently black. A survey was arranged with a company called Damp Detectives.[1] I have used them since and thoroughly recommend their sensible and professional approach to this sort of issue. (They work all over the country.) I attended personally when the survey was conducted, so I can relate accurately what was involved and what their conclusions were. This wasn't a 'look-see' by a builder who could then quote for some works which may or may not have been appropriate and insufficiently comprehensive. He used thermometers, hygrometers and other pieces of kit in order to arrive at scientifically proven conclusions.

He was able to establish that there was poor insulation to the sloping ceiling over the staircase. He established that the wall cavity was damp, and by inspection he determined that the roof void was so damp that the insulation was sodden. He also found that the extractor from the bathroom was ineffective and that there was no mechanical extraction from the kitchen section of the open plan living room. In this particular property there is a retaining wall adjoining the main house, without a vertical break to prevent the tracking of

---

1. See: www.dampdetectives.co.uk

water. The damp proof course was breached in several places by untidy mortar and the gable end wall pointing was in bad repair. There are a few other common contributory factors which on this occasion weren't part and parcel of the problem. For example, blocked drainpipes can result in overflowing water running down a wall which can lead to condensation problems and ageing roofing felt can mean that driving rain gets under roof tiles and enters the roof void. A contractor was engaged, and the following work carried out:

- The gable end wall was re-pointed.
- That wall was then treated with a coating which allows water vapour to escape but prevents further water ingress.
- A vertical gap was cut between the retaining wall and the main property wall.
- Small vents were fitted to the mortar of the walls at ground level, mid-level and high-level.
- Three roof vents were fitted either side of the property.
- Vents were fitted to the soffits around the property.
- Thick insulation plasterboard was fitted to the sloping ceiling and decorated.
- The bathroom extractor trunking was altered. Instead of running across the ceiling horizontally to a vent in the soffit, it was taken vertically to a new vent in the roof. This stopped the water vapour condensing in the aluminium conduit in the loft space, which had previously rendered the extractor useless.
- An identical extraction arrangement was installed in the kitchen area.
- Breaches in the damp penetration course (DPC) were cleaned.

The total cost of these works was around £2,800. Now this isn't an entirely insignificant sum by any means and in addition there were the costs associated with redecoration once the property had dried out sufficiently. There have been no further issues with condensation mould, however, and tenants have lived there without complaint ever since. His rents are now higher than they would have been, and he has experienced no costs associated with 'temporary fixes'.

Another Example: This Time Tenant-related

This example is also an extreme case, but for entirely different reasons. The property was probably built in the late-1990s and had been lived in without problem by the landlord's elderly mother for a good number of years. A series of tenants also then lived in the property without problems for a few years. A young couple with a child then moved in and, shortly thereafter, reports were made of 'damp' issues. The tenants claimed to be doing all the right things and indeed, at inspections, it looked as if windows were being opened, heating was being turned on and windows wiped down, etc.

Eventually, the tenant reported that the carpet in the bedroom 'squelched' when he walked over it. Since everything else appeared to be in order, a water leak was suspected. There was a part of the communal garden adjacent to the affected bedroom which was narrow and dark and that did not have much sun reach it. This area was coincidentally sodden, which lent more credence to the belief that there was a leak. The tenant was allowed to leave, without penalty, and moved into a property elsewhere after which two large dehumidifiers were installed and run for a couple of weeks. It really was that wet. They were then turned off and everyone waited for the leak to reveal itself. Eventually, it became apparent that there had been no such leak.

The property was redecorated and re-let, and no such issues have subsequently been reported. It's clear now that the young couple, with a child, had been doing everything wrong and managing to cover up their behaviour whenever someone visited the apartment. We'll never know precisely what they were doing, but drying wet clothes, running the washing machine as regularly as young parents are obliged to do, cooking with the windows shut, showering and not opening windows probably all contributed. And no doubt in a ground floor apartment, sleeping with windows closed (and who knows, maybe not even drawing the curtains unless a visit was expected) all probably played a part.

Conclusion

Tenant education, property design and maintenance together with regular visits are all factors concerning condensation mould.

CHAPTER 15

Preparing Your Property for Letting

When letting a property, thorough and adequate preparation is fundamental. I never cease to be amazed at how many landlords seem to forget about this, or leave it until the last minute, only to discover silly and often preventable issues they haven't dealt with. The tenant moves in and in no time at all is complaining about something or other. Before you arrange for the inventory to be drawn up (*Chapter 16*) make sure that the property has been cleaned from top to bottom. Whilst you may be prepared to accept a slightly dirty property when a tenant moves out, and you might have been easy on the outgoing tenant for some reason, your incoming tenant will want it squeaky clean. Would you want to find yourself having to vacuum or dust, or worse, on the first day in your new home?

It's not just the tenant that you need to be concerned about. If a deposit deduction goes to arbitration at the end of a tenancy, you'll need to provide the agreed inventory to substantiate your claim. When something is described as 'clean' it has to be just that. No dust, no dirt, no grime, no cobwebs. Then if it is handed back anything other than clean the difference is entirely obvious. If, however, as is sometimes the case, an inventory describes a shower screen as having 'small' or 'minor' watermarks, things start to become subjective. If it is left with watermarks following the tenancy are these smaller or larger than those originally present? What exactly is 'light debris' on a carpet, or 'tiny spots of burned on carbon deposits' in an oven? And you can bet that the adjudicator will find in the tenant's favour when the original description isn't clear. The following indicate the kind of action you can take:

- Ensure that all the lights are working and replace any lamps/bulbs as necessary.

- Take care of all those minor maintenance issues. The loose toilet seat, the broken blind, the ill-fitting trim on the kitchen cabinet, the wobbly curtain pole, the missing shower curtain hooks. Whatever it may be, please get it fixed.

- Look for any areas of decoration which could do with a touch up, or walls that need re-painting. I had a tenant move out of one of my properties and, in fairness, it could probably have gone another tenancy without redecoration. But I realised that if the new tenant stayed for any length of time (and it turns out that she has), either she would be living in a tired apartment, or I'd have to arrange for the works while she was living there, with all the upheaval that would cause her. So, while the place was empty, I arranged for a contractor to whip around with some emulsion. The new tenancy started off on a good note. She hadn't been expecting this extra care and it was obvious that redecoration had been carried out.

- Get the carpets professionally cleaned and make sure those few stubborn marks are removed. Are there any areas that would benefit from new carpets or vinyl?

- If you've had any condensation mould issues (*Chapter 14*), clean the affected areas, then use mould inhibitor and re-paint. Replace dirty, mouldy grouting and sealant. Apart from it being better that way, any evidence of mould at the start of a tenancy will count against you when it comes to claiming from a deposit at the end if matters have got worse. And don't forget the seals around windows and the areas behind front doors by the skirting board which are sometimes magnets for mould. Experienced tenants look for signs of condensation mould. Maybe they suffer with asthma or have had a bad experience previously having been blamed for allowing mould to develop in the past. If they suspect that a property is susceptible to mould, they'll probably move on to the next one they are booked to see.

- Make sure you get rid of any watermarks or limescale deposits. Bathrooms and kitchens, in particular benefit from a professional clean. And while a cleaner is dealing with those areas, why not get them to do the whole place? Your agent will be able to suggest good, reliable companies. The same cleaners can make dirty ovens and cookers look like new. It might cost another £50 or £60 but once again it will save no end of arguments during or at the end of the tenancy. Remember that when this comes around, if your tenant hasn't abided by your check-out guidelines and handed the property back in inventory condition, fair wear and tear excepted, you are quite within your rights to get the professional in to rectify it and charge the tenant for this. No matter what the overall cost is, if you do things properly from the start this should be the last time you need to fund such cleaning yourself. (And like all maintenance costs it will count against your tax liability later).

- Get rid of all the rubbish you have yourself been storing in the shed, roof space or garage. Do you really need those bits and pieces that are in the cupboard under the stairs? The fewer things you leave, the less will need to be itemised on the inventory and the tidier and more appealing the property will be. Empty your wheelie bins. Your tenant is bound to have rubbish to get rid of when he moves in, and he won't thank you for leaving his bins full. Once again, if you cause problems now, don't be surprised if your tenants aren't so keen to take away their rubbish when they leave.

- Windows are frequently overlooked. It might be argued that this isn't a hanging offence (depending upon exactly how dirty they are). Just make sure that if you are adopting a relaxed attitude to this now you will need to adopt exactly the same attitude when your tenant leaves.

- Don't forget the garden (*Chapter 13*). Mow the lawns, trim the edges, weed the flower beds, and cut back the hedges. Does the shed roof need re-felting? Is the latch on the garden gate working? Are there keys to any padlocks? Does the decking or patio need pressure-washing? Time-consuming though this may be, to leave it slippery is to invite an accident and a potential claim.

- Ensure that you have sufficient sets of keys. Give your tenant two complete sets (as recorded in the inventory), even if it's a single person; tenants have partners, parents, cleaners and all manner of people who might need access. If you need to cut keys, go to a reputable locksmith. With non-specialists their range of blanks is limited, and invariably in my experience cheaply produced keys are the ones that cause problems. But keep a complete set for yourself. If you use an agent, he'll also need one.

- Make sure that you leave instruction manuals and safety instructions for any appliances that you leave. This is a legal requirement. Photocopy them so that if your tenant 'loses' them they can easily be replaced.

- If you do not already have a current gas safety certificate, arrange for one to be carried out a few days in advance of the pre-tenancy clean and the start date. If the engineer comes across an issue, he'll need time to organize spare parts and this certificate is an absolute must. Under no circumstances should you allow a tenancy to begin without one.

- You'll also need an electrical safety inspection and Electrical Installation Condition Report (EICR) and any movable appliances you are providing will need portable appliance testing (PAT). As I say elsewhere in the book my advice is to remove or just provide as few as possible of these 'small devices' which tenants often prefer to replace with ones of their own choosing.

- Depending upon the age of your property, you may well end up with at least a few remedial works that (possibly legally) need sorting straightaway or within 28 days of the check in.

- A legionella risk-assessment is required under health and safety laws. You don't need to test the water, but you do need to carry out a risk-assessment. This doesn't need to be too onerous and, especially if you have no stored cold-water, it is something you're likely to be perfectly capable of doing yourself (see *Chapter 22*).

Our contractors are all fantastic, but they sometimes get their hands dirty and some of their boots and bags make a little mess. Ninety-nine per cent of the time they are quite good and clear up behind themselves, but you might want to check this after any works have been carried out, especially if the contractors aren't known to you. In a similar vein, contractors do not like using a property's toilet. There are occasions, however, when nature brings matters to a head.

Double-check loos don't need wiping or flushing. Leave some bleach, a toilet roll, and some paper towels just in case. Sometimes it's the smallest of things.

- Once all the works are complete, make sure that there is adequate time to prepare the inventory. Most properties can be done in half a day or less, but the larger the property and the more items you leave, the longer it will take. As advised in *Chapter 16,* please don't do this in the dark, and make sure that you have time to take good resolution photographs. Remember to allow time for everything to be proofed and printed out.
- If you've lived in the property yourself, remember to arrange for your mail to be re-directed. This takes a while to organize. Contact Royal Mail if you are unsure. This can be done online.[1]

---

1. See: www.royalmail.com/personal/receiving-mail/redirection

CHAPTER 16

Inventory, Tenancy Checks and Visits

The inventory, check-in, periodic visits by the landlord during a tenancy, and check-out share a common theme: to make sure that the property and its contents are in a good state when the tenancy starts, remain so allowing for fair wear and tear, and are returned in equivalent condition. In any dispute, arbitration or court proceedings concerning the tenant's deposit at the end of the tenancy the items discussed in this chapter will be all be relevant when considering whether that deposit should be forfeited in whole or part see *Chapter 21*.

The Inventory

The inventory is one of the four most important documents concerning a tenancy. Alongside the tenancy agreement (*Chapter 18*), electrical inspection condition report (EICR) and Gas Safety Certificate (both *Chapter 22*). It can seem time-consuming if it is done properly (or potentially expensive if done professionally), but its worth will be recognised in the event of a claim or dispute arising. The deposit is the tenant's money, and other things being equal he is entitled to ask for a full refund on leaving. A landlord can no longer make deductions with impunity. He must be in a position to prove that any claimed deductions are justifiable. The inventory is central to providing evidence to substantiate any such claim.

Remember my description of the inventories I had for my own 'accidental landlord' phase and the letting of my place in Dorchester? (*Chapter 1*). A few pages of typed notes and, whilst I don't remember the exact contents, I'm pretty certain it would have been something along the lines 'Living-room, white ceilings, magnolia walls, red curtains'. 'Bathroom, white suite, blue walls, black and white vinyl'. I see inventories like this with absolutely no reference to the condition of paintwork or carpets, no note of electrical sockets or other fixtures and fittings. The landlord is invariably pleased as punch because he did it himself and saved paying a fee. Irrespective of how pleased he is his tenant ought to be over the moon, since he can live almost exactly how he pleases with the landlord having virtually no recourse in the event of damages and dilapidations.

If your tenant has put a hole in a door, and the door wasn't described as being undamaged at the start of the tenancy, or if you cannot show a date stamped photograph, then you cannot prove that damage was his and the tenant can't easily be held liable. If the door isn't photographed and mentioned in the inventory at all, your tenant might even get away with removing it altogether!

Preparation and signing

A good quality inventory will contain an index for ease of reference for the adjudicator. Adjudicators seem to hate not being able to easily find a section to which they need to refer. Similarly, where images are used to illustrate a point, ensure that they are clearly referenced within the text. Adjudicators also dislike the use of acronyms. You may understand your coded shorthand, but an adjudicator is not at all interested in trying to decipher anything in an inventory, no matter how obvious you may believe it to be. Always base things on a worst-case scenario and assume that you're going to have problems when the tenant leaves. The more detail the better. For future inventories, you'll be able to copy and paste the bulk of the document, so it's only going to be painful the first time that you do it.

- At the beginning of the document, detail the location of the meters and any consumer units and stop cocks. Include meter references and images of the readings. List and have images of smoke and carbon monoxide (CO) detectors and have a statement to the effect that they are in working order. Get your tenant to sign to acknowledge that they were working at check-in (see later).
- Each room should be fully-described. It doesn't really matter how you do this but ensure that you have some consistency and explain things. If you start describing the walls clockwise from the door, say so, and

then do the same for each room. Don't leave any room for confusion, since, if it isn't clear, an adjudicator will find in the tenant's favour. It's a good idea to organize a flow for the individual room descriptions in advance of compiling the report. Ceilings, coving, walls, dado or picture rails, skirting boards, flooring, fireplaces, light fittings, electrical sockets, TV points, Sky or cable points, BT points. Separate each section with a sub-heading and make it clear and easily navigable.

- Each room should have an image showing the overall picture, so that an adjudicator may get a flavour of the total condition of a property. Where there's an area of damage or wear, include close-up images with a pencil, ruler or something to give an idea of scale. The description of each element should note the colour, finish and overall condition, and mention separately any individual blemish, marks or damage.

- In a kitchen, when describing the cabinets, start with either the wall units or the floor units and work in an organized manner. If you leave white goods, lawnmowers or vacuum cleaners, mention the brand and model number. If you have the serial number, include it. You must leave safety instructions for anything like this that you leave. Make sure these are noted individually in the inventory.

- Avoid descriptions which seem to indicate that everywhere is immaculate, unless of course it is. An inventory needs to fairly reflect the condition of the property and a tenant needs to sign to accept it. If you are at all biased in your description, the tenant will simply make amendments to the inventory and, were it to end up in dispute, it would be clear that you weren't being particularly accurate or fair.

It is often stated that an independent inventory clerk will produce the best inventory, and this will be looked upon in a better light in the event that an adjudicator needs to get involved. This may be true, so long as you engage the services of a reliable and large organization which will still be trading when your tenancy comes to an end. You will possibly need their assistance at that stage. Not all inventory clerks, however, are reliable or represent good value. The majority of independent companies (often one-man bands), tend to reduce their prices in order to secure work. All too often, they trade on price and not value. They are then having to carry out too many inventories in a day in order to make a living. There is surely a tendency to rush an inventory under these conditions and things are inevitably overlooked or badly worded. And, in winter months, you might find that your inventory is being prepared 'in the dark'. Good luck with describing a garden and the contents of an unlit shed under those conditions.

Place a disclaimer on the front which the tenant must sign saying that he has accepted the property as described unless he informs you in writing, within a week, of any discrepancies. You may have the time to run through it with him and he may be willing to spend an hour or so going around the property with you. But, if his furniture van is on the driveway and he's only rented it for half a day, he may well choose not to go through everything with you there and then.

Check-in

Agree in advance a time to meet with your tenant at the property. You should already have received the first month's rent and the deposit (with which you need to deal within 30 days of receipt: see below). Under no circumstances allow the tenancy to start unless you have cleared funds for the deposit and the rent. Do not hand over keys unless you have all the funds in your own hands/bank.

Your tenant should have been provided with a draft copy of the tenancy agreement in advance in order that he may check it and clarify any issues he comes across with you. If not yet done, get the tenancy agreement signed and witnessed, then date the agreement and hand over the keys. It's a good idea to get written confirmation that your tenant has received various documents required by law, and to obtain acknowledgement that things like stopcocks have been pointed out and demonstrated to be in working order. We use a simple sheet which the tenant initials illustrating acknowledgement of the following (you may of course feel it necessary to add to this list):

- How to rent booklet (provided at time of application).
- Deposit scheme terms and conditions.
- Legionella advice.
- Condensation mould advice.
- Gas safety certificate.

- Energy performance certificate (EPC).
- Electrical inspection condition report (EICR).
- Photo/photocopy of keys provided.
- Standing order mandate.
- Notes regarding reporting of the need for maintenance.
- Smoke detectors proved to be working.
- CO detectors proved to be working.
- Electric meter reading checked.
- Gas meter reading checked.
- Water meter reading checked.
- Location of stopcock.
- Stopcock working.
- Location of gas isolation valve pointed out.
- Location of consumer unit(s) pointed out.
- Inventory received.

My advice is to walk your tenant around, show him where everything is located. Explain any idiosyncrasies of the property and ensure that he is happy with the check-in. Also make sure that he has your contact details. Don't forget to inform the utility companies and the local council of the new tenancy. Otherwise, you'll continue to receive bills in your own name.

Periodic Visits

There are a hundred and one reasons why you really must carry out these important visits. Quite apart from it often being a term of an insurance policy or consent to let, you have legal obligations to which you need to adhere and some of these cannot be dealt with in the absence of visits. It's worth noting that in addition to the tenant's right to quiet and peaceful enjoyment of the property, he also has the legal right to exclude all others from his home, you included. You might have heard ill-informed talk of simply sending an email or a letter telling your tenant that you intend to visit.

Some people will tell you that you need to give 24, 48 or 72 hours' notice, depending on who you speak to, and that this is sufficient to allow you to turn up with your key and then take a good look around. Beware of adopting this approach. You *may* get away with it, but you could well be acting unlawfully. In fact, you need to get your tenant's express consent each time you wish to visit, irrespective of what terms you might have in your tenancy agreement. This means that you must write or send an email to your tenant and receive a reply telling you that this is acceptable to him. A telephone call might work but be careful if you have more than one tenant. The one with whom you spoke may not have told the other. The same is true of contractor visits, so ensure that your contractors also abide by this routine.

Tenants frequently wish to be present during any such visits, especially in the early days when they don't know you that well, haven't established a relationship and don't yet have the necessary degree of trust. Would you want a complete stranger wandering around your property in your absence? This might mean they need to take time off work, so ensure you attend when you have said that you will. Taking time off work effectively costs your tenant money and he won't necessarily wish to do this that often, so don't make the visits too frequent.

If a property is being well looked after and you have no concerns, then six monthly visits ought to be fine. Of course, if you discover an issue which needs some attention, then you may decide to make them more frequent. Your tenant ought to understand, however, that were it not for his actions you wouldn't feel the need to visit so regularly. Or, if the reason is property maintenance related, he might appreciate that you are trying to make his life more comfortable in some way.

One tale regarding a periodic visit
Having said that you need the express consent of a tenant, if you have a huge portfolio, like agents often do, the approach is sometimes altered slightly. It may be that an email is sent a couple of weeks in advance stating that a visit is being arranged for a Thursday morning and asking if the tenant would rather it was at a different time. If so, perhaps they would like to make contact and re-arrange. It may be that the agent then follows up with a text message a couple of days before, just to confirm the appointment once again offering the opportunity to change the timing.

Most of the time, this might work well, but a good agent will still appreciate that he is skating on thin ice. The agent will then turn up, assuming the tenant hasn't asked to re-arrange and knock on the door. He'll try and establish whether the tenant is at home, and if he is, he'll no doubt address the issue on the doorstep prior to entering. If not, he may use his own key thinking that the tenant knows of the visit and its purpose. If so, he will usually leave a business card or compliments slip in case he has inadvertently disturbed something, and the tenant realises that someone has been in his property.

I know of an occasion where an agent visited under exactly these circumstances, together with the property owner. The tenant wasn't at home, but unbeknown to anyone he had a video feed to his computer at work. The minute he realised that someone was in his living room he went home immediately to confront the 'intruder'. All ended well, but it serves to show that cutting corners can lead to problems. And as an aside, it also serves to illustrate that there are people out there with quite sophisticated approaches to personal security. So, if you're in your tenant's home alone, please don't go rifling through their belongings!

What should you be looking for?

There was a time when a visit was simply to make sure that the property was being well cared for. Sadly, those days are long gone and you nowadays have far more things to be concerned about. Yes, you will want to establish that your tenant is looking after the place and react to whatever you come across. Praise a tenant for looking after the place. All too often a common courtesy like this is overlooked. If you have issues, bring them up in as non-confrontational a manner as you can muster. Keep contemporaneous notes of findings and confirm in writing or by email anything that has been agreed. If you need to deal with a maintenance issue, do this as promptly as you can and confirm in writing your intentions and timescales.

Don't keep fobbing off a tenant, he may now report a landlord to the local council and you really won't want a visit from its officers, who will inevitably find far more issues of concern than either you or your tenant. A council issued improvement notice has time constraints under which you need to rectify issues (and you are unable to serve a Section 21 Notice until six months after rectification of any such works: *Chapter 22*).

Are you aware of the ramifications of additional and unexpected occupants? Whilst your tenant is allowed guests, make sure you are aware of any extra full-time occupants. A tenant has to have the legal right to be in the UK in order to have a tenancy and there are stringent checks to which you need to adhere. Whilst it may be the tenant who invited an illegal immigrant to move in, once you are aware, you have a legal duty to deal with the problem. Are you aware of regulations concerning homes in multiple occupation (HMOs)? Your tenant might have inadvertently, or knowingly, created an HMO and you as landlord will have to deal with the fallout. Whilst I will deal in more detail with legislation in *Chapter 22,* you need to be mindful of all manner of health and safety issues and should be casting an eye over the entire property looking for anything that might possibly create issues with which you'll be obliged to deal.

Check-out

Sometime in advance of the vacating date, provide your tenant with check-out guidelines. In that document, remind your tenant of his obligations. Quote clauses from your tenancy agreement if necessary. It's a good idea to provide contact details for any cleaners or gardeners you know who might be able to help. Remind your tenant of the need to dispose of the bulk of his rubbish, leaving a limited amount is acceptable though. Don't forget the garden and, if he has pets, he'll need to ensure any animal faeces are removed from there. Does he have an obligation to treat for pet fleas and dry-clean curtains? Much better to let him know what his obligations are in advance and to inform him of your expectations.

- It is always best to conduct a formal check-out at a time agreed with your tenant. It doesn't need to be the last day of the tenancy. You might wish to wait until the next day for any number of reasons, although it is prudent to ensure that the keys are collected on the last day and that meter readings are taken.
- If your tenant is present, then you might be able to come to an agreement on the condition of the property, its cleanliness etc. You might, however, have an uncomfortable relationship with him and wish to do this when he isn't present. If a tenant insists, it might be prudent to have somebody else with you.

- You don't necessarily have to agree to deductions there and then, you simply need to start negotiations in a timely manner. It may be that you need to get invoices or quotes for various works and unless you can come to some sort of deal without this, a tenant will have to accept a short delay while you gather prices.

- It's best to go through the inventory line-by-line and compare every element of the property as it is now to how it was described there. Just remember that you may not charge a tenant for fair wear and tear. Exactly what constitutes fair wear and tear will be determined by the length of the tenancy and the number of occupants. A single person having lived there for six years will undoubtedly have caused more wear and tear than a single person having lived there for six months. If you allow a family of five to move in, then expect more wear and tear than a couple who have been there for the same length of time. As a rule of thumb, marks to walls above waist height are probably excessive. Occasional marks below waist height are possibly fair wear and tear. The odd knock to a skirting board is common, gouges and lots of marks aren't. Marks to the ceiling are likely to be chargeable.

- When you go through the inventory line-by-line, use a copy and not the original. From your notes, compile a report in the same format as the inventory. You will need to provide a report if a dispute goes to arbitration. It is common for the inventory to have a column for check-out comments to make life easier.

- If your tenant is present, try and get agreement with your findings. He'll find it difficult to argue with you in the face of the original inventory which states that the carpets were clean, when you're standing in a room with wine stains or hair-straightener burns.

If you genuinely treat the issue of inventories, periodic visits, and the other processes described in this chapter properly, you will find that your tenancies and check-outs run far more smoothly than if you try to cut corners or save money.

CHAPTER 17

Insurance

There are three types of insurance the first two of which below are a necessity for a landlord the third highly advised.

The Building and Its Contents

If you own a leasehold property, then the insurance for the freehold structure will be paid by you through management charges or as a separate payment to the freeholder. Such insurance will be arranged and administered by him. If your property is freehold, then you'll need to insure it yourself. An existing domestic policy will not suffice, since the risks associated with a tenant are higher and the premiums are increased. Some of the perils that insurance can cover are of the kind I describe in other chapters where tenants have suffered loss, damage or injury. You will need to inform your insurers that the property is tenanted, or your insurance will be invalid.

Even if you are letting unfurnished, you'll probably want at least some contents cover, for things like curtains, carpets and white goods.

Liability

This will cover you in the event that your tenant slips on the decking you decided not to pressure-wash and needs expensive chiropractor manipulation. Or if he breaks a leg and can't work. Not having such cover isn't worth the risk nowadays. Remember my comment in *Chapter 13* about the injured tenant who is bound to have seen an advert on TV from an ambulance chasing firm of lawyers.

In 2013, a tenant had a kitchen cabinet fall off the wall. This cabinet was full of crockery which broke and, more importantly, it broke some of the tenant's teeth. Without going into great detail here, the landlord argued until he was blue in the face that it wasn't his problem and, only reluctantly, did he eventually settle with the tenant. It turns out that the cupboard had been fixed to the wall with entirely ill-suited fittings and had been a ticking time-bomb from then on. From memory, it was a few hundred pounds in dental bills and for crockery. But, God forbid, imagine if the picture had it fallen onto the young couple's baby who used to sleep in a basket under the cabinet.

A few times per year, we get spurious claims from tenants who seem to be wishing to cash in on something that has happened. At the time of writing, we have an ongoing dispute where the landlord does not have liability cover at all. I advised him to take independent legal advice in the face of a claim from a tenant of his and to date his lawyer's bill is in excess of £1,500. Liability cover would have cost a fraction of this and, in theory at least, the landlord continues to be exposed to a claim for damages that may run to over £10,000 in the event that his solicitor is unsuccessful in defending the action.

Rent Default Insurance

Assuming you have properly referenced a tenant to a proper standard (including financially speaking) and he has passed such tests, then this is an insurance product which may be available to you. Enquire before taking it out, however, to make sure that your referencing procedures are acceptable to the insurer you chose. Some insurers will take the premium but refuse to settle a claim because in the small print it is clearly stated that you must use a particular supplier for referencing. It is also the case that since Covid-19 began to impact some insurers have suspended this cover for new applicants or on renewal of existing policies. However it does seem that underwriters are now allowing such cover once again.

Generally speaking, these policies (some of which are attached to wider cover) offer to compensate you for unpaid rent and often cover legal fees, court costs and bailiffs' charges. They do vary and there will be small print, so be sure you look at the exact terms. Some have an excess—30 days' worth of rent is not particularly unusual. They all have a maximum sum that they will pay out, typically £25,000 or so, which is usually more than sufficient for the length of time it will take for lawyers to regain possession of your property. Some will also pay your rent until the property is fit to be re-let.

If you have a property of high value with an expensive rent, then be sure to bring this to the insurer's attention as you will probably be offered a slightly different product on more expensive terms. Costs vary but, as with anything, the cheapest is rarely going to be of much comfort to you in the event of a claim.

CHAPTER 18

Tenancy Agreements

I'm only going to discuss those common and routine types of agreements which I believe are most likely to be of interest to readers of this book. I am deliberately not going to describe pre-Housing Act 1988 tenancies, commercial leases, holiday lets, agricultural agreements, or less usual forms of tenancy that invariably require specialist advice. It is possible for a number of reasons, to use the wrong type of agreement. Please note that where this happens, by accident or design, if the tenancy were to lead to court proceedings, then the judge would have a discretion to treat the situation as if the correct type of agreement had been used. Ultimately there is little point, therefore, in deliberately using the wrong agreement. Everything I say in this chapter is subject to the Government's 2022 White Paper for a fairer private rental sector that I outline in *Chapter 22*.

Lodging Agreement/Licence

If a landlord lives on the premises, or where he lives, say, next door and the utilities are shared, this sort of agreement is appropriate. They don't really follow any given format. They are simply an agreement as to how things are intended to operate. The agreement might illustrate which rooms may be used, which shelf of a fridge, what days a washing machine will be free, the time by which the TV needs to be turned off, the arrangements for using the barbecue or swimming pool. You name it and it can probably be incorporated somewhere.

It's wise for such an agreement to have the rent stipulated, along with the term, whether it be three month, six months or whatever length is agreed. It ought also to have a provision covering the notice period that either party needs to give the other party. It's best for notice to be in writing. The agreement should clarify whether the rent includes the utilities (which is probably the best option), or alternatively, what formula is to be used to calculate the tenant's share. I deal with a relatively small number of these, and they are all entirely different.

Though preferable, there is no requirement that such an agreement be in writing. But good sense indicates that it is together with written receipts for rent paid and payments for bills made. Neither the landlord nor the tenant are bound by anything not agreed, the tenant acquires no other tenancy-related rights but whatever is agreed initially can be varied by agreement as time progresses.

Assured Shorthold Tenancy

The vast majority of tenancy agreements (including those we arrange are assured shorthold tenancies (ASTs). This may or may not be the case with you, depending upon your circumstances and target market. There are usually four main criteria for an agreement to be an AST:

- A rent of at least £250 and no more than £100,000 per annum.
- The tenant must be an individual, or several individuals. If your tenant is a limited company, you need to use a 'contractual agreement' (below).
- The tenant must have *exclusive use* of the whole or at least part the dwelling.
- The property must be the tenant's only or main residence.

Critically there are time constraints (but see Renewals below) that in turn are linked to the right to repossession. With AST's longer than six months these may if the parties so choose include a break clause allowing either the landlord or tenant to end their agreement during the fixed term, e.g. 12 months with a right to break the agreement after six months, whereby either can end the tenancy at that point. This provides both with a flexibility in case there is a change of circumstance or unforeseen *bona fide* problems arise.

A tenancy agreement should be a comprehensive document spelling out exactly what is intended between the parties. You don't need to be a solicitor to write one, but you should not even contemplate doing it yourself. By all means, look at examples online, but please ensure that you go to the trouble and expense of getting one from a reputable source.

It will list all of your obligations as a landlord, together with all those of the tenant. It is not uncommon for clauses to be developed over time following your own experiences. Here are four of a number of provisions that we have introduced following experiences that we have had (in a section headed 'Tenant Obligations'):

4.4.19   Not to introduce any water-bed into the Property without the Landlord's prior written consent.

4.3.30   Not to do any cutting or chopping directly on the work surfaces in the kitchen or mark in any way the work surfaces in the kitchen but to always use a chopping board for that purpose.

4.3.31   Not to hang wet towels or clothes over any doors. Damp articles left to dry on varnished or lacquered doors can cause mould marks to the woodwork. The Landlord reserves the right to repair, at the Tenant's expense, any doors where the finish has been damaged.

4.3.32   Not to hang coat hangers or similar over any doors. Such arrangements can mark the top of the door and the door frame. The Landlord reserves the right to repair any doors, at the Tenant's expense, where the finish has been damaged.

You'll notice that they are specific to problems already encountered that we wished to try and prevent in future. You can have any number of such clauses specific to your circumstances.

Statute law (*Chapter 22*) always trumps anything agreed in the sense that it prevents certain requirements as well as protecting both landlord and tenant. It lays down repairing obligations of the landlord so you cannot write a term in a tenancy agreement which override this. You cannot state that the tenant is responsible for repairing the roof. You cannot have a clause which makes the tenant responsible for the gas safety check on an appliance that you have supplied; and you cannot unlawfully discriminate. This is one reason for a landlord letting someone else deal with the drafting of a tenancy agreement. A solicitor, a landlord's association or a letting agent is perhaps the best source for these agreements, but even then you need to exercise a degree of caution. The law is complex and there are occasions where there are unintended consequences of electing to use one particular form of agreement, or for approaching a tenancy in a slightly different manner.

Statutory periodic tenancy

A statutory 'periodic tenancy' occurs when an AST ends without either the landlord giving notice or the tenant vacating at the end of its fixed term. There is no active renewal of the contract (see Renewals, below). The tenant simply stays on living in property. If he continues to pay rent and this is accepted by the landlord, the tenancy continues on a rolling, month-to-month, basis until either the landlord or tenant gives notice. There is flexibility, so that if the landlord decides that he wants the property back he can serve a Section 21 notice (whilst these last: see *Chapter 22*) or simply gain possession without having to wait for the remainder of a fixed term to expire. The tenant can give one month's notice on any rent day so in that respect he has greater freedom, but needs to balance this against what and when his landlord might do.

Contractual Tenancy

You might expect to come across these most often if you let to a company. For example, where a nationwide or international company decides to relocate a senior member of staff who has decided to rent your property the organization might take the tenancy in its own name, as opposed to giving an allowance to or reimbursing their employee to take out the tenancy.

The actual clauses within the tenancy agreement can be virtually identical to those of an AST (above). The deposit will be dealt with differently, but the obligations, responsibilities, do's and don'ts can be the same. Once again, ensure that you get this agreement from a reputable source.

Updating Agreements

I come across landlords who are using the same agreements that they were using five or ten years ago. We update our agreements and make changes on a regular basis. Legislation and case law often prompts changes, but so do our own experiences. It's a good idea to review these on a regular basis. Whilst you can't force a new agreement on a tenant midway through a tenancy, you should certainly review these between tenancies.

Renewals

An AST has what is called an initial fixed term. This might be for any length, but six or 12 months is not uncommon to begin with. If it is to exceed three years, then it must be dealt with by a solicitor by way of a 'deed'. The argument supporting an agreement for six months is that both parties get an opportunity to ensure they have made the right selection. There is little point is writing an agreement for less than six months, however, since a tenant cannot be forced out inside this period using a Section 21 Notice (see *Chapter 22*) and in the event of rent arrears, it is unlikely that possession will be granted within this timescale. And, of course, there are the costs associated with changing tenants which makes lesser terms uneconomic.

Thereafter, if nothing is specifically mentioned in the tenancy, it becomes 'statutory periodic tenancy' (above). The alternative is that the agreement states that it becomes a 'contractual periodic tenancy'. There may be good reasons why in your particular case a contractual tenancy or conversely a statutory periodic tenancy is best: please seek full advice. At the end of the initial fixed term, you are able to arrange for a renewal of the agreement, although you cannot increase rent in the first 12 months, unless you have a clause written into the initial agreement.

Renewal will provide both parties with some peace of mind and it is not unreasonable for either party to request one. The response of the other party may well be usefully revealing. There is, however, no compulsion to provide or suggest a renewal. In law, the tenant may stay *ad-infinitum* on the original six months' agreement from month-to-month and this is not detrimental in itself to either party. Indeed, it might be argued that with Section 21 Notices as things stand (and as long as they do *Chapter 22*), a landlord may more easily remove a troublesome tenant in a periodic phase.

Having a clause dealing with rent increases in the agreement means that they are easily dealt with, usually by negotiation in accordance with something like the Retail Price Index (RPI) or Consumer Price Index (CPI). By negotiation, I mean that if the RPI calculation works out at an increase of £26.93 you might decide to call it £20, £25 or £26.

When using an agent, however, be careful over renewals. This is an often unnecessary income stream for them and you may well be charged quite significant sums for this on an annual or even more regular basis. I used to employ someone who rented from a competitor and his landlord rang him one day to ask why he was leaving. He replied that he wasn't, but was informed by his landlord that his agent had informed him that he was indeed leaving. What had actually happened is that the tenant had turned down the opportunity of a renewal, since he now worked in a lettings agency and understood that there wasn't a particular need to renew.

The agent had intended serving notice on the tenant without the landlord's knowledge and then he would have benefited from another tenancy application fee from the landlord for having 'found' a tenant (and possibly to the tenant himself when these were lawful). If the tenant took out a fresh agreement the agent would make money for doing virtually nothing. If someone else rented the property the landlord would have suffered a void of some description and all the grief of an entirely unnecessary tenant find fee. Whilst tenant fee income is no longer a factor, nowadays the agent will still create additional turnover by charging the landlord for a new agreement. This isn't an isolated case and I know it happened to one landlord with a well-known agency.

If you do consider a renewal, I strongly urge you to insist on re-referencing and a fresh credit check. Not everyone does, but how else would you discover that your tenant had just lost his job, was under notice of redundancy, or had recently developed less than helpful spending habits?

Always Take Advice

If you have any doubt at all about the type of agreement to use, please take advice. Similarly, if there is anything in an agreement which you don't fully understand, ask someone who does. There are a variety of terms in a standard agreement (which is readily available, but easily misinterpreted). If you are serious about investing in properties, you really should make it your business to be thoroughly familiar with your obligations and your tenant's rights in particular.

In the next chapter, I discuss sub-letting and explain why it is troublesome. There are a multitude of problems which can crop up and which will cause the inexperienced or ill-equipped landlord difficulties.

CHAPTER 19

Sub-letting: Another Cautionary Note

In a leasehold property where you are the leaseholder, you are sub-letting to your tenant. But for the purpose of this chapter, I am referring to your tenant sub-letting to someone else entirely. This would mean that he has let out part (or even all) of the property to another person. Maybe he's renting out the second bedroom. If your tenancy agreement is silent on the subject (i.e. doesn't contain a 'no sub-letting' clause) then that tenant will need consent from you, but you can refuse for any reason.

If your tenancy agreement mentions sub-letting, you must ensure that the wording is accurate, since if your agreement states that consent is required and that the request will not be unreasonably withheld, then any reason for refusing must be reasonable. A term of your mortgage or insurance which prohibits this would be reasonable. This is a typical clause:

> 'Not to assign, underlet or part with or share possession of the whole or any part of the Property without the permission of the Landlord, such permission not to be unreasonably withheld.'

By having such a clause, you are highlighting the need for your tenant to seek consent from you. There are valid reasons why allowing the sub-letting of your property is not a good idea.

- It may be that you personally don't have a problem with a tenant letting a spare bedroom to a friend, but if you are ever asked to consider this sort of arrangement, take advice and ensure that you deal with all the various implications and enter into the arrangement with your eyes open.

- Don't just let a situation evolve and be passive about matters in the belief that it's entirely harmless. The sub-tenant (as a third-party) may not feel himself bound by your agreement with the tenant, not be creditworthy, in the country illegally, or 'scarper' leaving both you and the tenant high and dry.

My Experience of Sub-letting

A number of years ago, my agency acquired a portfolio of tenancies to manage, a handful of which were in the hands of a company which it transpired had sub-let to another limited company. All those landlords who had mortgages were exposed since, for a limited company, a contractual tenancy was in place and lenders invariably insist upon assured shorthold tenancies (ASTs). There were probably insurance considerations as well. The tenant who had sub-let was making a profit by charging a higher rent to the occupants, which meant that the landlord was not achieving the same level of rent he might have. Most importantly, however, was the loss of control. By their becoming involved in such a set-up, the landlords had no influence over the nature and identity of the occupants. The tenant was effectively choosing them according to his own criteria which may or may not have been as stringent as either our own, or those of the landlord. The occupants may not have been referenced to required standards and this would undoubtedly have invalidated any rental guarantee.

The landlords had absolutely no control over the nature of the occupants' agreements and the precise terms under which they were occupying the properties. For example, when it came to serving of notices, it transpired that they had an entirely different agreement with the tenant over their notice period. The genuine tenant believed that he knew all about lettings legislation, but it transpired that he was woefully ignorant and was effectively trying to use these landlords' properties as a means to get involved in 'rent-to-rent', an area which is fraught with danger for the unsuspecting. The affected properties suffered in terms of wear and tear and it proved to be troublesome and time-consuming to unpick the situation.

CHAPTER 20

Marketing

Without doubt, an agent has a far better reach than a private landlord when it comes to accessing Mr Blue-Chip. A good agent will advertise on all the main web portals as well as his own website. By my estimation, he'll stand a much better chance of a decent number of *quality* viewings than a landlord working independently; and with a knowledgeable and professional chance of targeting true market value. Even if you intend to *manage* the tenancy yourself, you would be well-advised to engage the services of an agent to secure a good quality tenant and ensure that he is robustly referenced including credit checking. The agent will make sure, e.g. that:

- The property is presented in the best possible light. Discuss this carefully with him when he comes to take his photographs.
- You tell him of your tenant profile.
- He fully understands what you see as the features and benefits of your property.
- There are proper and professional particulars. Make sure that you read these and sign them off. Are you happy with the text and the images he has produced? Is his description accurate and enticing?
- There is a good floor plan (something highly recommended).
- Any representations made about the property are valid and legal.
- The property is marketed at the correct price. I have covered elsewhere the folly of over-pricing and of 'knowing better' than an agent. I've also mentioned that the eventual (rather than the advertised) rent achieved for similar properties might not be apparent (*Chapter 6*). Take a long hard, look at these other properties and be honest with

yourself. Having considered all that I've mentioned across this book, is your property that different to others on the market at a lesser price than you are considering?

I say more about letting agent selection in *Chapter 23*, Expert Advice.

The Folly of Dual Marketing

Before the internet, agents had a prominent high street presence and it was important to be with the right one, to benefit from the footfall of a given location. Sometimes a landlord would market via joint agents, benefiting from visibility in different places. Nowadays, however, the internet makes an agent's physical location of secondary importance and marketing with more than one can in fact have a detrimental effect. There are good reasons for this, but perhaps the best of these is explained through an all-too-common problem we experience at application.

Someone will telephone an agent regarding a property that is being advertised. He'll tell him how many kids he has, what he does for a living and how much he earns. He will sometimes then tell the agent about his cat and dog. Once he realises that pets are not allowed, he'll sometimes say that he will 're-home' them and that 'it won't be a problem'. Are we really supposed to believe that pet lovers chop and change their animals according to circumstances in the way that we'd dispose of a wardrobe if a letting already has one? Unfortunately, I've been caught out by this. Whilst it may be that the minority of renters are spoiling things for the majority, I'm now reluctant to put this strategy to a landlord. No doubt all letting agents have had pets smuggled into properties against a landlord's wishes and it can cause trouble for all concerned (and may be in breach of the contract, or e.g. without 'the landlord's written consent' and subject to the cleaning of carpets before leaving: *Chapters 13* and *16*).

Now, suppose a landlord has instructed a second agent. Having learned his lesson with the first, the same person becomes a 'model applicant' and doesn't mention pets at all. A few weeks later, he moves in, and the pets simply vanish when periodic inspections are carried out. The landlord has been conned and has animals in his property, against his explicit wishes. You might argue that it's no big deal. But the landlord might only be letting temporarily and could have severe allergic reactions to pet hairs. Maybe a brand-new carpet is soiled and this only comes to light once the tenant has vacated. Smells can linger for inordinate periods of time. It might not be pets that cause the problem. The property might be inappropriate for the number of occupants that eventually live there. The wear and tear might be significant. The point is that were the property in the hands of a single agent this sort of thing would be far more easily detected and headed off at the pass.

Asking Too Much

Some while ago, we let a lovely property for a landlord and were lucky to obtain a rent at the top end. At the time, there was little else that compared with it. Recently, this self-managing landlord let us know (at the last minute) that the tenant had served notice. Against our better judgement, in a slow market, he demanded that it be re-marketed at the same price. The market was not as buoyant as it had been when we last let the property and the asking rent was predictably £100 too much. Despite regular calls during which he was advised to reduce the rent he was looking for, he stuck to his guns and the property remained empty for a prolonged period. Eventually, he decided, without even telling us, to instruct another agent. In line with our usual stance, we dis-instructed ourselves.

We wouldn't have been surprised if he accepted an offer from a model applicant once he'd learned his lesson with us. He might have got the asking price, but more than he bargained for. Had he taken our sensible advice, any number of applicants who viewed his property but then applied for others because his was overpriced might have applied to us for his. His property would have been let a month or so earlier and he'd only be maybe £100 a month worse off. He actually lost £2,000 in rent, which he may never make up. And he might have ended up with a less than honest tenant, together with the associated trouble.

Another Real Life Case

I had a different case where a perfectly decent applicant failed referencing. He thought he had a way around it, however. He would apply in his adult son's name and move in as a 'permitted occupier'. We were unable to allow this to happen, since we knew the circumstances, but were it to have been marketed by another agent he may well have used this ruse. The landlord might then have ended up with an occupier who was unable to pass referencing as a tenant (the father) after the adult son decided to move out.

Guaranteed Rent

Some agencies advertise that they'll pay your rent whether or not there is a tenant. For the uninitiated, this might seem like a good idea. But there are pitfalls.

- **Lower than market rent** If the agent is going to take the risk of paying you the rent regardless of whether the property is occupied, there's a good chance that he won't be getting you the best possible rent. He will just want to let the property as soon as possible to save money.
- **Agency fees** You will more than likely have to pay all his advertised fees in full and sometimes in advance. Forget about having the opportunity to negotiate a discount.
- **Shorter void periods** As already indicated, an agent who guarantees rent will be keen to have a tenant in situ as fast as he can (including whenever the tenancy changes) so void periods are minimised. This means that apart from the risk of him keeping the rent low (above) there will be less time to conduct inspections, prepare the inventory, carry out maintenance, cleaning, etc. (see in particular *Chapter 16*).
- **Quality of tenant** If an agent knows that he'll be paying you rent from his own pocket, he'll surely be tempted to spend less time securing the right quality of tenant. The first willing participant is likely to end up living in your property

CHAPTER 21

Deposits

For any assured shorthold tenancy (AST) (*Chapter 18*) (and since April 2007) tenants' deposits should be secured in one of the ways outlined below.

How to Deal With a Deposit

There are two ways of doing this as a landlord (or letting agent). You may:

- keep the deposit yourself and insure it. Where you keep it in your own account, you'll benefit from any interest accrued. But, with interest rates as low as they have been for some years (as of mid-2022) deposit interest is negligible and probably won't cover the cost of the insurance premiums. If at the end of the tenancy the landlord does not release the deposit, the insurance will pay back the tenant (and will then be free to chase the landlord); or
- transfer it to a bank account in the name of a Government sanctioned scheme, i.e. the Deposit Protection Service (DPS) (www.depositprotection.com), My Deposits (www.mydeposits.co.uk), or the Tenancy Deposit Scheme (www.tenancydepositscheme.com). Here interest is not generally paid to you, but with the DPS there is a free to use alternative dispute resolution (ADR) offer.

Deposit Schemes

I have no experience of keeping deposits personally and insuring them. All my own deposits are lodged in a custodial scheme. My experience is with the DPS and much of what I say in this chapter is based upon experiences with this scheme alone. There may be different rules and procedures with the other providers which you can easily check and compare. Further details can be found at their respective websites above.

Whatever solution you choose, you will need to ensure that you conform to the terms of the scheme as well as deposit legislation. You/your managing agent will need to serve prescribed information (PI) on your tenant within 30 days of receiving the deposit. This tells him about the deposit protection measures taken, the scheme's contact details, and the procedures that apply regarding protection and return of the deposit.

Failure to deal with a deposit correctly can result in harsh penalties. A court can demand its immediate return, as well as ordering the landlord to pay up to three times the value of the deposit to the tenant. It can also allow the tenant to stay on at the end of the tenancy. The statutory requirements are contained in the Housing Act 2004 (as amended) and they are summarised at www.gov.uk/tenancy-deposit-protection.

What is the Deposit For?

In broad terms the deposit is held by the landlord (whether or not in a scheme) against loss or damage caused by the tenant during the tenancy. Most tenancy agreements will stipulate that there are certain obligations on the tenant, including to look after the premises and report faults to the landlord/managing agent within a reasonable time or straightway if urgent. He should as described in *Chapter 13* behave 'in a tenant-like manner' and return the premises to the landlord in the same order as when the letting began. This is closely linked to having a proper inventory as explained in *Chapter 16*. At check-out any loss or damage during the tenancy must be agreed between the landlord and tenant. Failing this, the matter will if a dispute cannot be resolved end up going to arbitration or in extreme situations (e.g. where the damage far exceeds the deposit) a civil court for breach of contract. You should also be aware that occasionally tenants 'disappear' or fail to respond as you or I might, so that chasing them becomes a chore (even if most are keen to behave reasonably and partly because of what is due to them, or need a future reference from you).

An Example of Landlord Who Was 'Caught Out'

A few years ago, a landlord telephoned me to explain his circumstances and seek my advice. He'd privately let a plush two-bed apartment to a tenant who was in no way related to Mr Blue Chip. He'd taken a deposit, but not lodged it in time and he'd not supplied the PI (above) to the tenant. The tenant started complaining about all manner of issues, but also behaved oddly even refusing to allow access to a gas engineer to check the boiler. The landlord was made to return the deposit and to pay the tenant a penalty equivalent to twice its value. The tenant then continued to live in the property for about another year, until such time as we as agents could encourage him to leave. By which time, belatedly, the landlord had decided to instruct us to manage the tenancy.

When the tenant finally vacated, he made absolutely no attempt to clean the apartment. He had caused all manner of irritating minor damage and the apartment required full redecoration. The entire issue left the landlord with a bitter taste in his mouth. He ended up selling the property and has no intention of getting involved in letting again. It could have all been so different. Had he correctly referenced the tenant, he would have had a better chance of securing a reasonable one. Had he dealt with the deposit correctly, he'd have saved himself £2,000 and had recourse within his is own control for the damage caused. And, had the tenant not been able to live there without being subject to a properly dealt with deposit, he'd probably have looked after the place better and cleaned up before he left to ensure its return.

How Much Should the Deposit Be?

At about the time tenancy arrangement fees charged by letting agencies were banned, myriad deposit alternatives sprang up. Those promoting such schemes will tell you that it makes it easier for a tenant to afford to move. They will also tell you that you as a landlord to get the benefit of the (previously normal) deposit equal to *six weeks' rent* (and sometimes more). The tenant fee ban (above) now limits deposits to the equivalent of *five weeks' rent*. At first glance, therefore, these alternative schemes sound effective, and the take-up has, by all accounts, been good. In 2019 however, the Property Ombudsman reported that they were getting a growing number of complaints. And I suggest that, as more use is made of these schemes, these complaints will only increase. It seems that tenants haven't necessarily had matters fully-explained to them in relation to some schemes, and over the term of the tenancy the tenant will have paid far more in fees than he would have done were he to have paid the old-style traditional deposit. Furthermore, these fees are non-refundable, whilst the tenant is still liable for damages, dilapidations, cleaning, etc. The lack of transparency means that some tenants seem to believe damage no longer matters, since they are paying these regular non-refundable charges. Somehow, they are unaware that they will be relentlessly pursued for costs once the tenancy has ended.

Your tenant's financial position should concern you. And that you have a tenant in your property who is sooner or later unhappy and not overly bothered about looking after your property ought to worry you. In my opinion, a tenant with some 'skin in the game' is more likely to look after your property. If his landlord controls upwards of £1,000 of the tenant's money, there is surely far more chance of there being a happy outcome at check-out.

The agent selling such a scheme to both the landlord and the tenant is paid a referral fee equivalent to maybe a week or so's rent. I'm not sure that it is in their best financial interests to spell out fully the potential pitfalls of such schemes. And some agents pay their staff based upon fee income, so you can bet that individual negotiators will work tirelessly to sell these schemes. Otherwise apart from deposits being slightly smaller than they once were, nothing has changed with the traditional deposit idea which has largely served us all well for decades. If it ain't broke, don't go mending it.

Lifetime Deposits

This is a concept which is being considered and so is still in its infancy. In theory, since 51% of tenants receive their deposit back in full and 77% receive some of it back, the belief is that a scheme can be arrived at where deposits are somehow passed from one landlord to the next, thereby eliminating the need for a tenant to raise a new deposit whilst awaiting the return of the previous one. I hope that some sort of resolution may be arrived at, since finding a second deposit is often sufficient grounds for a tenant staying put in sometimes inappropriate accommodation. Expanding young families may well find moving causes financial hardship. My suspicion is that this will be a while in coming and that it may necessitate the involvement of the insurance industry and perhaps Parliament.

Deposit Deduction Disputes

If a deposit claim does go to arbitration, you don't have to have an invoice for a claim to be successful; a quotation for works is fine. You will need to provide the tenancy agreement to demonstrate that the tenant is responsible for the damage and that he's supposed to return the property in inventory condition, fair wear and tear excepted. After all, you might have let a tenant live there on a cheap rent and said to him that you didn't much care how it is handed back, since you intended to demolish the place. It's not your tenant's fault that you have changed your mind.

You'll need to provide a copy of the inventory, together with any supporting documentation and images (see again *Chapter 16* about the importance of taking photographs at the start of the tenancy). This might include periodic visit reports, copies of correspondence with the tenant where he accepts responsibility for damage, copies of quotations, original purchase receipts and indeed anything else that strengthens your hand. Have as many clear date stamped images as you can to help illustrate the exact nature and extent of the disputed damage. The more information you are able to provide and the more clearly it is presented, the more likely you are to be successful in your claim. Please note that you are unlikely to be successful in any claim for your own time or travel expenses in pursuing the claim.

The DPS released data in late-2019 showing that 43% of tenants agree to some form of deduction from their deposit and that rent arrears and property cleaning are the most common reasons.

My Show Home Landlord

This is the same the chap I told you about who had fancy wallpaper on his staircase. He had tenants who stayed for around a year. They looked after his home well and it was virtually immaculate, with the exception of the skirting boards. The tenants had an upright vacuum cleaner and at the end of very sweep it seems that the skirting board was hit, leaving black rubber marks, about 15 mm above the floor. If I'm honest, this was new to me, having never come across this particular issue before. The skirting was coated with a white gloss paint, so it wasn't as if an inappropriate one had been used. But, in their endeavours to maintain a clean and tidy home, the tenants had inadvertently caused damage to it.

On this occasion, the landlord claimed for the entire redecoration of the skirting boards. In fairness, he had a decorator who didn't charge a ridiculous sum and the tenants agreed, albeit somewhat reluctantly. I've subsequently been introduced to a 'miracle cleaning paste' called Pink Stuff.[1] It turns out that this removes such marks with ease.

Strictly speaking, the landlord was wrong to charge his tenants because of legal principle known as 'betterment'. This basically establishes that someone may not be in a better position following resolution of a problem than he would have been were the issue not to have arisen. By insisting on brand new paintwork throughout the skirting, he had effectively wound the clock back to the time when it was last painted a number of years previously. He should, in my opinion, have sought compensation for a proportion of the work. Had he enjoyed five years' use from the skirting boards and were such paintwork to have a life of, for argument's sake, eight years, then he should have claimed

---

1.   See: www.thepinkstuff.co.uk

just 3/8 of the total cost. The time by which the need to repaint was cut short. That's assuming of course that this was the tenants' damage. It was settled by negotiation, but I would like to have heard the response of the adjudicator.

Other issues are rather more cut-and-dried. A coal falls from a fire and damages the carpet for example. (Let's say 0.05% of the total area to be generous). The carpet has a lifespan of ten years and is five years old. It cost £1,000, so it is now worth £500. This might mean that the landlord's percentage loss amounts to just a few pence. In cases such as these, a compensation sum may be sought, depending upon the size of the burn. Typically £25 or £50 would be accepted were it to go to dispute. A landlord seeking the entire £1,000 for a new carpet would be unlikely to succeed and might even find himself being awarded nothing. That carpet at today's prices might be £1,250 and I know of landlords who have tried to use a deposit to cover replacement on a like-for-like basis. Naturally they were unsuccessful.

The Lottery that is Arbitration

Quite apart from the time, trouble and expense you expend when a claim is disputed, you will be exposed to the vagaries of arbitration, and you won't always arrive at a reasonable and acceptable end as you see it. This is why negotiating with a tenant, even if you are left feeling slightly out of pocket, is the better course of action. You or the tenant can always choose the courts as an alternative to arbitration with one of the scheme providers. What needs to be borne in mind, however, is that the courts deal with far fewer of these claims than the schemes and are much less familiar with the terms of an agreement. In my experience, resolution through a scheme is the better of two unfortunate choices.

In quick succession, I had experience of two check-outs in identical apartments, on the same side of the same block, both of which had condensation mould issues and both entirely down to the tenants' lifestyles (see *Chapter 14*). Not only was there mould on walls, furniture, curtains and window reveals and soffits, but the tenants had shown absolutely no willingness to even attempt to clean it away. The ADR Scheme of the DPS received virtually identical evidence from each landlord, and both cases were disputed by the tenants. In one, the landlord was successful and achieved a payout (from the deposit) of some £400. The other tenant was rather more vociferous in his defence and wrote particularly eloquently of the propensity for condensation mould in UK homes and the potential risk to occupants in affected properties. His landlord received nothing. Coincidentally, a year or two before, a Finish family tried unsuccessfully to counter a claim under similar circumstances and in a similarly eloquent fashion. The claim on that occasion was for considerably more and involved redecoration works. I trust that you are beginning to realise that a well-prepared inventory is not a waste of time or expense after all.

An Extreme Example of Woe

We took over a tenancy which had been arranged by another agent. Towards the end of the tenancy, it was discovered that the entire property had been badly redecorated by the tenants. Furthermore, a bedroom wall had been stripped and then plastered, once again badly. And, for some inexplicable reason, laminate flooring had been poorly fitted over the top of carpet in the same bedroom. What had been white woodwork was now chocolate brown or turquoise; it varied from room-to-room. Wallpaper had been badly hung in the living room. The house had not been cleaned and the garden was full of rubbish. Concrete slabs had been laid on the front lawn to enable an additional vehicle to be parked there.

The situation was slightly more complicated, in that we didn't at first understand that any work had been carried out by the tenants, having not seen the property originally, and having not received an inventory when the property was handed over to us. Our periodic visit clerk just assumed that it was 'one of those properties'. A number we took over when we bought this portfolio were guilty of falling into this category. Almost by chance, we discovered during a conversation with the owner that the home had been in perfect order when the tenants moved in, and that the decoration was entirely neutral at that time. Before the end of the tenancy, we had a frank conversation with the tenants who assured us that they would put everything back as it was. Sadly, it transpired that their idea of returning it to its original condition involved simply repainting with no preparatory work at all.

The previous agent hadn't made an inventory and had not carried out any periodic visits. Whether or not the agent had consented to redecoration works is unclear, but had he done so, it was without the landlord's knowledge or agreement. Purely by chance, two contractors we engaged to quote for redecoration works and cleaning had been involved in the preparation of the property just before the tenancy started. Both were able to provide copy invoices to verify this. Again, by chance, the landlord had photographs of the property, taken just before the tenants moved in. When all this was added together, there was sufficient evidence to dispute matters, were it to go that far.

Fortunately, the tenants capitulated at the last minute and, in return for the landlord not pursuing them for the balance of the costs, they agreed to release the full £1,600 deposit to the landlord. The landlord was still left out-of-pocket, but it was not the straw to break that particular camel's back. It was the inevitable price of not doing things properly. The inexperienced landlord chose an agent without doing too much research (see *Chapter 23*). The agent failed spectacularly in his duties. The tenants were left to their own devices. Nothing but the little bit of good fortune at the end was ever going to save this landlord from a much worse outcome.

CHAPTER 22

The Law of Landlord and Tenant

As a landlord you are subject to the general law depending on the part of the UK involved. I focus on England and Wales in this chapter and those special provisions which lawyers categorise as 'The Law of Landlord and Tenant'.

General law comprises common law and legislation, the latter created by Parliament and comprising (1) statutes (aka 'Acts of Parliament' or 'primary legislation') and (2) regulations (usually) made by Ministers of State (aka subordinate', 'secondary' or 'delegated' legislation). You also need to be aware of another kind of subordinate legislation: local by laws that might affect residential letting in your own area.

Ignorance of the law is no excuse, even though some criminal offences attract 'strict liability' (without fault) or are hard to understand. By contrast, most serious offences require intention, negligence or knowledge (*mens rea*) and a high standard of proof. There is then the civil law that governs contracts (including tenancy agreements) and private rights. Finally, you need to keep an eye on compliance officers charged with ensuring public safety.

You'll be liable directly to your tenant, his family, his visitors, etc. for any injury, loss or damage due to your legal shortcomings. As well as neighbours, passers-by and in some cases even trespassers.

Fortunately, there is good news. Courts (and to an extent all public bodies) must act fairly, reasonably and without discrimination. Plus, you can take out insurance for civil (but not criminal) hazards (*Chapter 17*). And in many situations, you may have a defence if you inspected periodically (*Chapter 16*), took action, or warned your tenant about something. But if he touches a badly maintained light switch, or smoke alarms have not been maintained, or his guest trips over a frayed carpet, you could find yourself in trouble, even in prison for causing unlawful injury (or worse). If you store prohibited data, or don't declare rent to the tax man (money laundering: see later in this chapter), you risk a heavy financial penalty and costs. Or you may get a fixed penalty notice for lesser transgressions.

The Law of Landlord and Tenant is an ever-changing feast, on which books have been written, entire careers built, and websites overflow. Nonetheless, you need to understand the basics, most of which won't change tomorrow. Here in this chapter I suggest steps you can take to limit or avoid problems. In essence, you are 'supplying' your tenant with his home and possibly white goods, appliances, and maybe furniture. All must be safe and fit for purpose in every respect. My main advice is that you should be as careful as possible, act in a timely way if an issue arises and reasonably at all times. Please also be aware of laws mentioned in other chapters. And remember: only the foolhardy will contemplate being involved in this marketplace without expert assistance.

Homes (Fitness for Human Habitation) Act 2018

Under this legislation, which incorporates the Housing Health and Safety Rating System (HHSRS) you are basically tasked with ensuring that your tenant's home is safe in every regard. You might regard this as a 'catch-all' piece of legislation.

I have already covered your repairing obligations (*Chapter 13*) and the initial preparation of your property (*Chapter 15*). Regular inspections (*Chapter 16*) together with the prompt and effective responses to issues uncovered or reported by your tenant is key. Burying your head in the sand serves no useful purpose, since as I have already said ignorance is no defence in the eyes of the law.

According to this legislation, there are 29 areas of concern (referred to in the industry as '29 ways to kill your tenant'!). The risks are divided into four different areas:

Physiological
Damp and mould, excessively cold temperatures, excessively hot temperatures, asbestos, biocides (damp treatments for example), carbon monoxide dangers, lead, radiation, unburned fuel, gas, volatile organic compounds.

Psychological

Overcrowding or lack of space, entry by intruders, lighting, noise.

Infection

Domestic hygiene, pests/refuse, food safety, personal hygiene, sanitation/drainage, water supply for domestic use.

Accident

Falls associated with baths/showers, falling on a level surface, falls on steps/stairs, falls between levels, electrical hazards, fires/flames/hot surfaces, collision and entrapments, explosion, position and operability of amenities, structural collapse/failings.

The importance of this piece of legislation cannot be over-emphasised. Local authorities have a duty to follow up on reports or complaints by tenants and will take it upon themselves to act when they come across issues themselves through advertisements or elsewhere. Ignoring any potential issue and certainly by not reacting to reports from your tenant will leave you exposed to improvement notices, fines and in the extreme, a banning order.

A Common Often Overlooked Example

Building regulations generally have a purpose. In the case of a staircase, there are maximum distances that are allowed between the upright banister supports or similar. This is so that a child is unable to put his head between them and then trip with his head caught. I have lost count of the number of times that I have come across situations where some are removed for aesthetic reasons. I have also come across staircases where there is either no banister at all, or where the last few steps have no banister.

Where it is a house you live in yourself, that's one thing, but where you have tenants with children, or who might one day have children, or who might have friends with children, then it is potentially a ticking time-bomb. And it's not just children that might potentially cause you problems. What of the frail or slightly inebriated tenant who stumbles on such a construction when wending his way home 'by rail' following an enthusiastic night on the tiles?

I've solved this problem on a number of occasions, and it really shouldn't be that big a deal. It is typical, however, of the sort of problem which can exist in a home without a landlord even being aware of the issue.

And even worse still...

A couple of years back, I came across a staircase that had come away from the wall, with the actual steps falling away entirely. It transpires that at some stage, someone had decided that the staircase would look better without a number of stringers under each step. It was these stringers which held the staircase together and over time, it all fell apart. A young child was living there at the time and were he to have been on the stairs at the time, the result could have been much worse than it was. This was in the days before this legislation and the tenant wasn't tempted to report it to the local council.

The landlord, however, adopted quite an unusual stance. Rather than immediately rectify the problem, he suggested that the tenants use a ladder for 'a couple of days' whilst he sought a solution. He was forced to accept that this was totally unacceptable and, fortunately, the tenants were able to stay with family members for two days whilst a new staircase was fitted.

Any property you are going to let out needs to be fully surveyed with care. You need to take into account every conceivable danger and seek advice where necessary to ensure that you eliminate anything of a safety concern prior to letting anyone move in. If you consider that you are not up to the task, get a lettings agent to take a look for you. Information on the internet may point you in the right direction. If you come across something which is a cause for concern, don't brush it under the carpet. If you already own the property, get someone in to give you a quote to rectify the issues. If you don't yet own it, how much will putting it right cost you? Is there an alternative property where the works aren't required? Even where this specific piece of legislation doesn't cover something, your tenants are going to be protected under consumer protection legislation.

GDPR and the Information Commissioner

Since you are controlling and processing data belonging to your tenant, you may need to register with (or satisfy) the Information Commmissioner's Office (ICO). For full details of this obligations, see www.ico.org.uk. There is a fee for registration which in 2022 is £40 per annum or £35 if you elect to pay by direct debit. Fines for data breaches can be extreme and are based upon a percentage of your annual turnover. You need to ensure that any contractors you use also treat your data properly.

Registration of Landlords

This is something which is not yet a requirement in England, but will become so within the near future. Until full details are released, nobody knows for certain what this will entail. There are already requirements for registration in both Scotland and Wales and it is likely that English registration will follow along similar lines. Sooner or later, if you are operating as a landlord in England, then you will need to comply with a registration scheme of some description. Failure to do so will undoubtedly result in harsh penalties.

Retaliatory Eviction and the Deregulation Act 2015

Retaliatory eviction is where a tenant makes a legitimate complaint to a landlord about the condition of his property and, in response, instead of making the repair, a landlord serves him with an eviction notice. The Government, quite rightly regards retaliatory eviction as an unacceptable practice and considers that tenants should not fear becoming homeless because they have made a necessary request.

Where a tenant has a genuine concern about the condition of your property they are able to make a complaint to the local council. The local authority can serve an improvement notice or a notice of emergency remedial action, and you will not be able to use a Section 21 Notice (see later) to evict that tenant for six months from the date that such repairs have been completed.

Under any circumstances, you would be well-advised to keep a paper trail of any reports of maintenance and any actions that you have taken to remedy the problem. Even if the council hasn't been approached, it's best practice to keep such records.

Improvement notices

Where your tenant complains to the local council about a particular issue, the council will visit your property. Since the council Inspector will understand far more about housing issues than your tenant, the inspector will nowadays undertake a complete inspection. Your tenant may have only complained about something to which you haven't reacted, but the council may well end up with a much longer list of issues with which you will be obliged to comply.

A recent example

I came across a situation recently which demonstrates this issue quite clearly. Someone within the local council was searching through online adverts in an attempt to find housing suited to tenants the council was seeking to house. He saw an advert for a property being advertised without heating. This was then reported to the improvement officer. A visit followed and, in addition to the heating concerns, three further (on this occasion minor) issues were added to a list which the landlord was sent, together with a deadline by which they needed to be resolved. In some parts of the country, local authorities are more pro-active than in others. Nowadays, penalties levied may be kept by the local authority and some it seems are arguably far more likely to uncover issues and levy fines.

Right to Rent

You now have to ensure that anyone over the age of 18 who is living in your property has the legal right to live in the UK. You are not allowed to assume that someone is British and are obliged to prove that every single tenant is either a British National or has the right to be in the UK. This involves taking and retaining an original copy of a passport or visa or, if a British citizen doesn't have a passport, a birth certificate and photographic identification (ID).

A tenant's visa only needs to be valid at the start of the tenancy. If, however, it expires after the tenancy starts, you are obliged to check at 12 months that they have renewed it. If they have not, you are legally obliged to inform the Home Office.

Under certain circumstances, you may be obliged to seek possession of the property. You would be well-advised to take advice if you are at all unsure of your legal obligations, since once again, there are stiff penalties for not complying. Bear in mind that dependent children may well turn 18 during the course of a tenancy and you are equally obliged to ensure that they also have the right to be in the UK. You are probably unaware that you also have obligations under the Immigration (Hotel Records) Order 1972, to keep records of any occupants over the age of 16. It is likely that the age requirements will be lowered to as young as 12 years of age.

Gas Safety (Installation and Use) Regulations 1996/1998

In short, you must have any gas appliances checked annually and provide your tenant with a copy of the certificate within 28 days of the check (and before the start of any tenancy). You must retain a copy of this for two years.

A new installation will have a commissioning certificate which is acceptable for a period of 12 months from installation, after which annuals checks must be carried out and certificates provided. Naturally, there is much more to this legislation. Fines under it can be £5,000 per offence, so if you have a number of breaches, the total can be huge. And you can also go to jail for six months.

Electrical Equipment Regulations

Recent legislation means that you are now legally obliged to have the electrical installations of your property inspected every five years. Any remedial works must be attended to within 28 days. You will need an electrical installation condition report (EICR) from a suitably qualified electrician.

Separate and in addition to the EICR and proof of any remedial work, any portable appliances must also be tested (PAT = portable appliance testing).

This in itself is one reason why a growing number of landlords have decided to stop providing portable goods to their tenants.

There are also checks that you are required to conduct between tenancies. You are responsible for checking the leads, plugs and fuses on white goods that you supply. This will inevitably involve dragging appliances from under work-tops in order to access the leads, plugs and fuses.

Fire Safety of Furniture and Furnishings

The Furniture and Furnishings (Fire) (Safety) Regulations 1988 mean that as a 'supplier' of furniture, you are obliged to ensure that it meets the requirements of legislation. Articles covered must have labels attached which confirm compliance. You should keep receipts and proof of compliance.

Legionella

Since 2013, landlords have been obliged to conduct legionella risk-assessments. This does not usually involve the actual testing of the water supply. It is simply an assessment of the water supply. In order to comply with the legislation you will need to ensure that the water from taps is either suitably hot or cold: that where any cold water is stored in a tank it has a secure, tight fitting lid and is not suffering from rust or sludge or residue build-up of any description. You must ensure that when your tenant moves in, any shower heads or water diffusers to taps are clean.

If there is any redundant pipework where water may stand and stagnate, this must be capped off or removed. If you have a 'jacuzzi' style bath or hot-tub, then you will need to take advice and provide your tenants with clear instructions on how they are to avoid risk. You also need to take outside taps into consideration .

Your tenant must be provided with a copy of this assessment. A good tenancy agreement will pass to your tenant the obligation to ensure that showerheads are kept clean and to report issues regarding inadequate water temperatures. Periodic assessments will be necessary and in any case you would be well-advised to carry out a fresh assessment in the event that you have a vulnerable tenant move in or if one of your existing tenants becomes vulnerable in health terms. In most cases, a periodic inspection may well be every two or three years. For some further advice see the Government website: www.hse.gov.uk/legionnaires/

Non-Resident Tax

Are you going overseas for more than six months? If so, you will need to register with Her Majesty's Revenue & Customs (HMRC) in order to receive your rents without the deduction of tax. Nowadays you may register online and the process is quite straightforward.[1] If you use an agent, you will need their unique reference prior to applying and will need to notify HMRC if you change agent.

If you don't register and don't use an agent, then your tenant is supposed to deduct tax and report this to HMRC. Whilst tenants may not be aware of this, they won't be happy if it is brought to their attention by a helpful friend.

Homes in Multiple Occupation

There are rafts of legislation concerning homes in multiple occupation (HMOs) and I don't intend to cover it all here. Suffice it to say that if you have a property with more than one family occupying it, then you need to look into this in more detail.[2] Three or more individuals in a property comprising two or more families will mean that you are likely to have an HMO of some description, whether it be licensable or non-licensable. In some parts of the country, an 'Article 4 planning directive' will be in place and this means that whilst it is a non-licensable HMO, you will still need planning consent. Such consent will ordinarily be conditional upon provision of additional fire and safety features. Linked smoke detectors, fire-doors, fire-blankets etc. are typical requirements.

---

1. See www.gov.uk/guidance/paying-tax-on-rent-to-landlords-abroad
2. See www.gov.uk/private-renting/houses-in-multiple-occupation

Minimum Energy Efficiency Standard (MEES)

It has been a legal requirement to have an energy performance certificate (EPC) prior to marketing a property for sale or rent for some years now. EPCS are valid for ten years. For any new tenancies starting after 1 April 2020, the property must have a minimum E rating. Under certain circumstances you may register for exemption. There may be grants available for some works that might be required. There may also be temporary exemptions for new landlords which may be applicable, depending upon circumstances.

If a property doesn't have a minimum E rating, then it is likely to be cold, suffer drafts, and will be expensive to heat. If you don't already own the property, then unless there is good reason for investing in one such as this, you are probably best advised to continue your search for something more appropriate.

Money Laundering

You should be aware that HM Revenue & Customs (in particular) but also other authorities and professionals have by law become quite pro-active concerning money laundering. Solicitors, accountants and, e.g. banks, insurance companies and even ordinary traders are required by law to report 'suspicious financial activity'. This also applies to lettings agents and to you as a landlord. Naturally, you need to make an annual tax return, but you also need to understand where your tenant's money comes from. It is far better to have a trace of this using bank transfers as nowadays even relatively small amounts of cash, certainly anything above £1,000 in cash, should put you on enquiry, especially if there are other circumstances indicative of criminal proceeds, such as drugs, unusually high consumption of energy, or disproportionate or unexplained amounts of ready money in the hands of say a benefits claimant or other 'breadline tenant'. And of course keeping money 'under the bed' is a bad move for either you or your tenant.

The Government White Paper

In June 2022 the Government published a White Paper, 'A Fairer Private Rented Sector'[3] containing proposals for the biggest shake-up in decades of residential lettings law. These plans would, among other things, extend a Decent Homes Standard to private residential lettings and create a Private Renters' Ombudsman whose role would include settling disputes, thus avoiding the undoubted stress and confrontational nature of court processes (which Government promises it would in any event reform and accelerate). Once debated, these innovations are scheduled for inclusion in a Renters' Reform Bill that would:

- convert assured shorthold tenancies (ASTs) into periodic tenancies;
- allow these to be terminated by the tenant with two months' notice or by landlords with a 'legitimate reason' (including that he wishes *bona fide* to sell that rental property;
- abolish (a) Section 21 notices (above) in favour of fresh grounds of possession; (b) rent review clauses (whilst retaining the possibility of controlled annual increases); and (c) blanket bans on renting to families with children or refusing tenancies to tenants on benefits;
- encourage landlords to accept pets (subject to insurance);
- create a property portal to support renters and weed out 'rogues'; and
- make local authorities more accountable for housing standards.

It may be that these or further changes will codify other legal requirements concerning private sector rentals but only time will tell.

---

3. See: www.gov.uk/government/publications/a-fairer-private-rented-sector

CHAPTER 23

Expert Advice

Quite apart from legal advice (*Chapter 22*) there are other sources of informed professional and practical advice about letting property. You might be tempted to take advice from a friend or 'uncle' who is a landlord. This is perfectly natural and you are bound to listen to this, and may well begin to make your decisions based upon it. However, I'd urge a degree of caution. Things have moved on remarkably in the lettings industry. Certain practices which would have perfectly acceptable in the past are now no longer acceptable, frowned upon or even unlawful. The family friend might be a 'great landlord', but he may have had his properties and tenants for some while. Were his property to become available tomorrow, he might be in for a shock.

Please don't base your decisions solely upon the word of someone who may be out of touch. He may have struck it lucky, had uncomplaining tenants who have put up with a lesser quality home whilst their children went through their schooling. Or perhaps they were first time tenants with few expectations. There are any number of reasons why your friend's circumstances might be unusual. Even if he is doing pretty well, maybe with up to ten properties, this really isn't much exposure to the market on which to base a meaningful opinion. A successful agent will have hundreds of homes under management from which to draw his experience and opinions. Needless to say, he'll also have regular contact with others from whom you should seek advice: lawyers, accountants, builders, cleaners, etc.

Selecting an Agent

I've already mentioned different types of agent in *Chapter 6*. Choosing an agent with whom to begin a meaningful long-term business relationship is perhaps the most difficult choice you will need to make. I come into contact with many through training courses, breakfast meetings with solicitors to discuss legal changes, online forums and our own company's networking group. I'm aware of variations in skills, experience, diligence and approaches to customer service. I don't envy you your task. I believe I am pretty knowledgeable and can see that few readers will really have the understanding or contacts to embark upon letting property without the aid of a good agent. Don't let this deter you. They do exist, but you need to find them.

Years ago, I met a landlord who ended up leaving his 'wonderful' property empty because he couldn't accept the risks associated with letting. When I was called to value it, I visited and took details of comparable offerings which I might or not take out of my briefcase depending upon what I found. What I *did* find was unexpected, an inhabitable cellar that wasn't obvious from the street. I also found a similarly useful loft conversion. The property had a fantastic bathroom and kitchen, bespoke cabinets in the dining-room, a fitted wine-cooler, similar cabinetry in the living room, and the entire downstairs was wired for sound with speakers set into the ceilings. My comparable properties stayed put. Other agents, however, turned up with nicely typed out valuation letters. Maybe they were telepathic? Ironically, after a couple of years, the landlord came back to us to manage his tenancy and it has all gone rather well. I understand that he didn't get in touch with the other agents who'd assumed a valuation in advance from just their external impressions.

I recently took a call from an 'accidental' landlord (*Chapter 1*). That he called himself accidental spoke volumes. He'd already been talking with others in the industry and it transpired he'd indeed spoken with five before me. I know this because he told me of the five different valuations he'd received for his property over the telephone. I don't know about you, but if I wanted an extension to my house and I called a builder, I'd expect him to take a look before giving me a price. Why should it be different with a letting proposition?

I was asked, 'How do you organize maintenance?' 'Will you charge a commission on contractor's invoices?' 'How do you ensure the right quality of tenant?'

'I've been told it would be ideal for sharers, what are your thoughts?' The list of questions was virtually endless. I asked him who had recommended us as agents and was told it was glowing reviews on the internet that prompted the call. He asked sensible questions and only towards the end did we get around to fees. At that stage I explained that until I'd seen the property, understood his expectations in terms of our involvement and the rent, and got a feel for the whole situation, I wouldn't be in a position to comment. I was the sole agent invited to see his property and I listed it a few days later.

You are about to allow an agent to take partial control of a valuable asset. Even if capable of managing the letting yourself, you are enabling him to help in the determination of a tenant. Does he know a good tenant from a bad one? What's his track record? It must surely be tempting for some agents to save better tenants for those tenancies they manage themselves and palm off lesser ones on those who only want them to find the tenant. And, even if the agent only does that, even if the tenant is Mr Blue-Chip, how can you be certain that the correct legal processes will be followed to allow you to gain possession of your property at a time of your choosing some time in the future? To start with, it's important to understand the differences in the various kinds of letting agents operating in the marketplace.

1. Corporate

As the title suggests, this agent will be part of a significant corporate body, ultimately answerable to shareholders and profit driven. There is absolutely nothing wrong with a business seeking to profit from its activities, but sometimes there is a culture which permeates down to the branch and creates local profit-driven challenges. They will be system-orientated which in many ways is a good. There will be staff within the business with a good grasp of relevant legislation (*Chapter 22*) and best practice. There will undoubtedly be good training structures in place, and they will offer their staff a career path.

You might well find, however, that there are centralised call-centres for certain functions. Accounting may be dealt with remotely and, when you have a query, you are dealing with it by telephone with someone who has never even been to your town, let alone property. It may well be that they sub-contract certain functions, such as inventories, periodic visits and check-outs. That's all well and good when things go well, but when you do have a problem you are once again dealing with someone by telephone. And sub-contractors carry-out such work at a price and the companies used change with annoying regularity. When you have a deposit dispute, the information simply isn't there, and it may be that nobody really cares, since it doesn't affect them directly. Systems work, but they are not necessarily there to ensure the best outcome for the landlord, or indeed the tenant. They are tick-box exercises to ensure that procedures are adhered to.

What of local staff turnover? Somebody somewhere knows and understands you, but are they within the branch that is looking after your affairs? The career path is great for staff, but does it leave void periods which are often covered by ill-trained or temporary staff? Are they all sufficiently motivated to want to ensure that your need is paramount? As an aside, we recently hired someone who had previously worked for a corporate agency. He was quite a good negotiator and property lister, but a long way from the finished article. He enjoyed working for us but, after a little over a year, was enticed back by the corporate agent to work as their manager. It was great news for us, since we had a real handle on what was going on with them and their standards, but I'm not so sure that their customers were as happy about his new responsibilities.

2. Local Independent

This agent may well have been around for years. He's probably got a successful team of staff and a quite significant portfolio of properties. In a largely unregulated industry such as property letting, it's possible for someone to have been trading for years without the need to keep abreast of legislation. Until recently, there was no need for an agent to have client money protection or to be a member of a redress scheme. Some such agents are fantastic. I know of many throughout the country who take a pride in doing things professionally, expediently, and transparently. By the same token, there are others who are living on borrowed time. In June 2019, tenant fees were banned and overnight every agent in the country lost a large proportion of their cash turnover. The majority have now adjusted their business model to compensate, but there are a few that acted like rabbits caught in headlights and have done little if anything to compensate.

To put this in perspective, it has been suggested that every agent in the country who hasn't made sensible adjustments to their business has lost his entire profit through that change in the law. Some agents (among them independents) are simply hoping to pick up additional business as if this will somehow make up for their lost revenues. When the sales market has slowed in the past, it was only natural for agents to embark upon letting. A number have, therefore, ended up in a sector of the industry not by desire so much as necessity.

3. Franchises

Similar to local independents, these are locally owned and managed, but they benefit from the back-up of a national brand. In addition to the branding, their franchisor offers training, mentoring, a framework of procedures to follow, legislative assistance and regular advice and support. You can be pretty certain that a franchise will have CMP in place and be a member of a redress scheme. Also, that they will audit their branches at least annually.

4. Online agents

As I write this, I'm wondering just how long it will take for this book to be completed. If it's too long, this section might end up being a history lesson, since I personally don't believe that online agents can survive much longer. For a minute, let's forget about the online property sales agent. I'm specifically refer- ring to online letting agents. Their model is quite simple. Because they don't have offices, they are supposedly able to make huge savings which they pass on to their customers. But we're not discussing Ocado or Amazon supplying baked beans or books, we're talking of someone sitting in a room somewhere, purporting to be able to do exactly the same as those in a fully staffed office. They will tell you that they offer an online proposition that somehow a physi- cal high-street presence cannot.

The online agents, however, advertise on the same portals as high street agents and high street agents have their own large and busy websites, often with far more useful information contained in them. Online agents can arrange view- ings 24/7, so can those wishing to view properties. But a growing number of high street agents are also able to do this. Established high street agents are also able to have tenants report maintenance and other issues through mobile phone apps. They have portals which enable landlords and tenants to view their accounts. And high street agents already use sophisticated software to aid in the preparation of inventories, periodic visit reports, check-ins and check- outs (*Chapter 16*).

In short, the online agents don't generally offer anything that a high street agent is unable to offer. What they are able to offer you, however, is a real headache when it comes to wanting to confront them face-to-face in the event of there being a problem. If getting the cheapest and least transparent of agents is your sole aim, then maybe they are the answer, but if you're taking your investment seriously this is one area where you really shouldn't cut corners.

Questions to Ask Agents

We all buy from people we like and, indeed, I often find myself saying that 'I set my stall out and attract like-minded individuals'. This is true, but please don't use an agent simply because you like him. And don't do what I did in Dorchester and use an agent simply because you met him at the local pub. Do some research. Much of this you should be able to get with a little hunting online.

Before you approach the agent, check out their online reviews. Reviews are becoming more and more prevalent and are often a really useful resource for when you are making any decision to make a purchase and my industry is no different. Simply 'Google' the agent's name and town and you should start seeing results. It might also be worth checking them out (e.g. at www.viewagents. com or their Facebook page). Unless they have an obvious external feed to their website, beware of reviews which have been uploaded to their own website. Whilst I'm sure that they will be genuine and unadulterated, are they really going to show the bad ones? Much has been made of certain review platforms lately which, seemingly, allow the removal of less attractive reviews. I personally believe that every business eventually encounters an unhappy customer and a lack of negative reviews to me is something of a red-flag. I also believe that a review says as much about the reviewer as the company it is reviewing. Often the response from the business owner enables the reader to draw sensible conclusions about possible bad motivation for a review. It will also shed light on the agent's way of dealing with matters. At his website, you'll possibly see details on staffing levels and, with luck, come across blogs which may well throw some light on their attitudes to all manner of property-related issues. What about the agent's Facebook page? Once again, you'll get an impression of the sort of company you are considering dealing with. Employers use this when considering candidates for employment and it's a legitimate way of carrying out research on companies. Here are some questions for your agent:

- How many tenancies does he manage? The scale of his outfit or branch will show whether he is a serious player in the market.
- Is he VAT registered? There are agents out there who aren't. This is indicative of their smaller size. At the time of writing, VAT registration is required for a turnover of £85,000 and above (This will equate to a portfolio size in the South of England of around 50 properties).
- How many full-time staff does he employ? One portfolio we bought came from a company run by the principal and two part-timers. There were regularly notes fixed to the door ('On a viewing, back in 15 minutes', etc.) Both you and your tenants/prospective tenants will need to be able to get hold of the agent during office hours. And enough staff are required to look after a portfolio properly.
- Where is he based in relation to your property? Major cities and rural locations will have their own demands, but just how much time will the agent be able to spend at your property and how much time will be spent travelling to and from it? This is particularly important when there are maintenance or other problems with which to deal.
- How much rent can I expect? Is the agent prepared to provide you with a valuation over the telephone? I've already made my views on remote answers without viewing the property abundantly clear. So now you should discover for yourself his approach.
- What exactly are his fees? You are likely to get some sort of answer, but this isn't really that important a question at this stage. You need to be trying to establish whether or not you like his approach to things. Can you work with him? When the subject of fees does eventually get raised, there is an oft-quoted adage in the industry: 'A good agent isn't necessarily cheap, and a cheap agent isn't necessarily good'. It's trite and it gets bounced around at trade conferences and training courses, but there is an awful lot of truth to it. If the agent is prepared to negotiate immediately on his fees, how likely do you think it is that he will negotiate well on your behalf when it comes to rent increases, deposit deductions, etc? Many agents have a scale of fees, management

charges and extras, which they may tailor to your situation, and you should be able see these in writing.

- What office and other hours does the agent keep? Again, it's indicative of whether it's a serious business.
- Which sort of properties does he deal with? Is he really the appropriate agent for your property? Does he have relevant experience of your type of property?
- Does he have CMP? It's been a legal requirement for a while, but even so some agents are still trading without it. This insurance covers your money and that of your tenant in the event of misappropriation by the company or its staff.
- What redress scheme is he a member of? Agents have to be members of a redress scheme. This gives customers the right to redress through independent third parties for any grievances you might have with a member agent. Not being a member is one thing, but if an agent is thrown out of one scheme he is unable to join another. So has he been expelled from a scheme already?
- Does he pay rents to landlords every working day of the year, or just weekly, monthly? Your rent is far better in your account than his.
- What is his record of rent arrears? The national average is around 13%, but in areas with low unemployment this should be low or non-existent. If he doesn't know, or he is hesitant in answering, you may draw your own conclusions.
- What systems does he have for recording and monitoring maintenance? You need to be confident that an agent deals with the maintenance of your asset professionally and expediently and has systems to support it. How much involvement can you personally expect in maintenance decisions? A regular complaint I hear of agents concerns spending a landlord's money with little or no thought or negotiation.
- What steps does he take to ensure that only the right tenants are introduced to your property? By now, you should have a pretty good idea of what to expect as an answer.
- What is his policy on periodic inspection visits? Hopefully you have a good handle on this now also. In what format is his visit report?

It's no longer acceptable to receive a three paragraph letter explaining that 'all is well'. You should receive a proper report detailing the findings, together with embedded images. This will prove crucial if there is a deposit dispute (*Chapter 20*). Ask to see an example of an inventory and a periodic visit report. He will be able to redact any personal information. This will tell you if he sub-contracts and will certainly show you how he approaches the issue.

- What is his approach to deposit disputes? How will he fight your corner? Will you be charged an additional fee for this service?
- What is his policy with regard to legionella risk-assessments? (*Chapter 22*). Some agents will insist on entirely unnecessary and unduly expensive testing. But landlords often discover issues with cold water tanks and pipes which would have resulted in significant leaks and damage were it not that such basic structural checks were correctly carried out.

Check the agent's terms of business concerning your termination of the agreement. It's not unusual for an agent to try and tell you that the tenant is *his* and that you cannot terminate while the tenancy continues. This is not the case, the tenant is *yours* and the contract is between you and the tenant. He might have found a tenant for you, but if he doesn't perform you should be able to dis-instruct him without losing your tenant. Equitable terms of business will have a notice period or a payment equivalent to that notice period's fees. Three or four months might be deemed fair. A month's rent plus VAT is also not uncommon and is not entirely disproportionate. If you have negotiated a huge discount and simply want to try and wriggle out of an agreement afterwards, then expect there to be more of a penalty for seeking to break it. In February 2022, a large corporate had a landlord take it to court over such a clause. It was found that there was insufficient detail in the terms of business concerning the landlord's ability to terminate and thousands of their landlords are now able to leave without difficulty in the event that they are dissatisfied.

Ask to see his terms of business which you will be expected to sign. Ensure that you fully-understand them. Pay special regard to any terms which involve you taking responsibility for anything. Having an agent doesn't absolve you of all legal responsibility, but if you're expecting a fully-managed tenancy service ensure that the agent will be doing everything you are expecting of him. If you were to take your car to a number of main dealers to have it serviced, you can be pretty certain that all the garages would carry out the same tasks. One or two might provide a courtesy car or give away free mints, but the actual service would be identical. This is not the case with letting agents' offerings They all differ and the way to establish what the differences are is to read the terms of business and query what you discover.

To Bear in Mind If Thinking of 'Going it Alone'

You'll know what your tenant looks like and he'll know you. You will have his contact details and he will have yours. And that's fine isn't it? Whenever I go to Tesco for my shopping, I'm amazed at the number of people I bump into that I know personally. I often see some I recognise when I am out to dinner or going to the cinema. Once in a while, my wife and I bump into tenants of ours, although since I no longer have day-to-day contact with them, they rarely know who I am. I believe, however, that sometimes the planets align and consequently landlords bump into tenants when it's far from convenient. You're all dressed-up in your finery and meeting friends or work colleagues or, heaven forbid, customers you know through your job, and you bump into a tenant as he sways up the high street, slightly the worse for wear. He's glad to have bumped into you, since he's been trying to get hold of you for days to find out about those repairs you promised. Such conversations are rarely short and civilised. It's easy for my wife and I to deal with. Our office is open Monday morning, and we'll deal with it then. For you, however, you have no office or shop-front and your tenant will want to sort it out right there and then.

In addition to having the skills and experience of an agent to insulate you, an agent will provide you with the comfort of anonymity. Even if you don't bump into your tenant, he'll ring you when you're at a party or watching TV or putting the kids to bed. Fancy having to deal with a pilot light that won't stay alight when you're at Gatwick, queuing for your flight? Or would it be better to wait until you get to your hotel in some foreign resort to sort out an emergency plumber to stop the water running down your staircase?

Epilogue

I haven't covered every single aspect of letting property in this book. I dare say that it would be impossible to allow for each eventuality and, even were I to attempt this, by the time I'd have finished things would have marched on, thanks to changes in legislation, technology, fashion or building regulations, to name but a few variables. With luck, however, I've scratched sufficient of the surface for you to now appreciate that there is a lot more to renting out property than meets the eye, but that a prudent and well-researched approach, sensibly funded, has every chance of success. By now, you will know what sort of land-lord you are, you'll have figured out how much you can afford and have the basics to enable you to approach this subject professionally and dispassionately.

Thanks for taking the time to read the book and I hope that it has proved worthwhile. I wish you all the very best in your endeavours, whether caused by a temporary move overseas or a fervent desire to build your own property empire.

Index

A

abuse of property *37*
accidents *37, 195*
advice *31, 205–214*
'A Fairer Private Rented Sector'.
    See *fairness*
agents *179–182*
  franchises *209*
  online agents *209*
  sale agents *65–70*
  sole agent *74*
airing cupboard *130*
annexes *89, 95*
arbitration *155, 187*
arm's length *35, 67, 83*
asbestos *194*
assistance dog. See *pets: assistance dog*
assured shorthold tenancy. See *tenancy:*
    assured shorthold tenancy
auctions *69*
availability *83*

B

bathrooms *112–117*
betterment *188*
bias *157*
biocides *194*
blinds *128*

Blue-Chip. See *tenants: 'Mr Blue-Chip'*
boilers *117*
  combination boiler *130*
break clause *170*
budget *34, 43–52*
building *165*
  building regulations *195*
bus stops *99, 104*
buy-to-let *43, 46*

C

cannabis farm *40*
carbon monoxide *132, 156, 194*
  carbon monoxide detector *50, 132*
carpets *112–114*
caution *76, 172, 177*
ceramics *112*
character properties *99*
check-in/check-out *155–164*
children *86, 134, 195*
cleanliness *90*
cleats *128*
cold *194*
colour scheme *111, 195*
communication *39*
compliance *66, 193*
compromise *140*
condensation mould *141–148, 189*

consent *79, 191*

   consent to let *43, 53*

   homes in multiple occupation *201*

contact details *159*

contents *165*

contingency *50–51*

contract

   contractors *160*

   contractual tenancy. See *tenancy: contractual tenancy*

conveyancing *31*

costs *22, 46, 50, 77, 108*

   running costs *98*

council tax *51*

courtesy *161*

Covid-19 *36, 46*

credit checks *83, 174*

curtains *128, 128–130*

D

damage *41, 90, 157, 184*

damp *147, 194.* See also *condensation mould*

danger *196*

decking *134, 165*

décor *22, 110, 190*

   redecoration *191*

deeds *31, 173*

dehumidifier *142*

demand *35*

deposit *115, 127, 155, 183–192*

   deductions *163*

design *123*

detached properties *99*

detectors *132, 156*

dilapidations *186*

disability *88*

discrimination *88*

   age discrimination *77*

disharmony *96*

disputes *96, 155*

   alternative dispute resolution *183*

double-glazing *92, 145*

downstairs *97*

drives *136*

due diligence *69*

durability *113*

E

electrics *51, 121, 124, 131, 159, 195, 199*

emotion *25, 101*

employment *83*

energy *202*

   energy performance certificate *50, 159, 202*

equity *29*

eviction *41, 197*

   retaliatory eviction *197*

extractor fans *142*

F

facilities *101*

fairness

   'A Fairer Private Rented Sector' *198*

   fair expectations *109*

   fair wear and tear *115, 155, 163, 187*

families *116*

faults *184*

fences *136*

finance *65*

fire *38, 40, 61, 195, 200, 201*

  fire prevention *80*

  open fires *131*

flood *38, 103, 142*

floors *112*

  parquet flooring *114*

flowerbeds *135*

freehold *31, 53, 165*

  management *54*

funding *33*

furniture *90, 108, 144*

  storage *23*

G

garage *92*

garden *90, 99, 133–140*

gas *125, 138, 194*

  bottled gas *132*

  gas fires *130–131*

  gas isolation valve *159*

  gas safety *50, 158, 199*

GDPR *197*

Government *46, 197, 203*

greenhouse *134*

Grenfell disaster *61*

grievances *96*

ground rent. See *rent: ground rent*

grouting *119*

guarantor *76, 80*

H

hallways *113*

health and safety *162, 194*

heating *98, 130–132, 142, 194, 198*

  air-source heating *130*

  central heating *92*

hedges *135*

hobs *125*

Homes (Fitness for Human Habitation) Act 2018 *194*

honesty *37*

house *91*

  house in multiple occupation *80, 162*

  Housing Act 1988 *169*

  Housing Act 2004 *184*

  housing benefit *77, 88*

humidity *142*

hygiene *112, 119, 195*

I

immigration *199*

improvement notice *161, 197*

infection *195*

Information Commissioner's Office *197*

ingress protection *122*

inheritance tax *31*

inspection *199, 212*

insulation *145*

insurance *41, 50, 56, 103, 159, 165–168*

interest rates *46–52, 72*

interference *137*

intrusion *161*

inventory *24, 90, 155–164, 187*

investment *33*

  bricks and mortar *25*

  larger properties *93*

K

keys *158*

  window keys *133*

kitchen *122–125*, *157*

  kitchen flooring *112*

L

laminate *114*, *190*

landlord

  access by *136*

  accidental landlord *21*

  Landlord and Tenant Act 1985 *138*

  landlord's consent *40*

  lucky landlord *25*

  registration *197*

Land Registry *31*, *74*

law *193–204*

lawns *135*

lead *194*

leasehold *31*, *165*

  Leasehold Reform (Ground Rent) Act
    2022 *56*

legionella *51*, *158*, *200*

leveraging *47*

licence to occupy *169*

lifestyle *79*, *141*

lifts *62*

lighting *127*, *195*

  LED lighting *127*

like-for-like *139*

linen *108*

living room *113*

loans *45*

location *35*, *72*, *75*, *101–106*

lodgings *169*

loft *137*

loss *184*

luck *33*

M

maintenance *22*, *83*, *141*, *159–160*, *212*

maisonette *54*

management

  self-managing *96*, *181*, *214*

market *107*, *205*

  marketing *179*

    dual marketing *180*

  market value *79*, *179*

  rental market *35*

mattresses *108*

maturity *76*

meters *159*

mobility *97*

moisture *143*

money

  client money protection *208*

  money laundering *202*

mortgage *43*

motivation *26*

mould *158*, *194*. See also *condensation
    mould*

N

naïvety *24*

noise *98*, *195*

notice

  Section 8 notice *38*

  Section 21 notice *38*, *161*, *203*

  to vacate *38*

O

occupants *161*

oven *125*

P

paintwork *111*

parking *91, 101, 105*

particulars *179*

patios *135*

periodic visits. See *visits*

pets *85, 180*

  assistance dog *86*

photographs *156, 179*

planning permission *80, 93*

ponds *133*

population *102*

portable appliance testing *199*

possession *38, 170*

Premium Bonds *34*

prevention *123*

price *179*

profit *41, 73*

property

  property sizes *89*

  property type *35*

  sourcing property *65*

prudence *46*

Q

quality *123, 205*

quiet enjoyment *137, 159*

R

race *88*

radiation *194*

radiators *120*

railway stations *104*

redecoration. See *décor*

referencing *36, 41, 76, 87, 174, 185*

refurbishment *36, 50*

reliability *37*

religion *88*

renewal *173*

rent

  double rent *39*

  first month's rent *158*

  ground rent *55–56*

  rental expectations *73–74*

  rental insurance *166*

  rent default *37*

  Renters' Reform Bill *203*

  rent increase *174*

  right to rent *198*

repairs *109, 115, 171, 194, 197*

replacements *138*

repossession. See *possession*

reserves *36*

respect *29*

Retaliatory Eviction and the Deregula-tion Act 2015 *197*

retro-fittings *117*

Rightmove *65, 68, 89*

risk *33–42, 46, 206*

  risk-assessments *200*

road network *106*

rubbish *162, 190, 195*

S

safety *121, 133, 138, 201*

  safety instructions *157*

sanitation *138, 195*

schools *98, 101, 102*

sealant *119*

secondment *81*

Section 8 notice. See *notice: Section 8 notice*

Section 21 notice. See *notice: Section 21 notice*

security *98, 137, 161*

semi-detached houses *98*

sexual orientation *88*

Shamplina, Paul *33*

shops *103*

smoke detector *50, 132, 159*

sockets *126, 157*

solicitor *32*

splashbacks *124*

staircases *195*

Stamp Duty Land Tax *31, 50*

stepping back *26*

stopcocks *158*

storage *91, 108, 110, 136*

    kitchen storage *122*

structure *138*

students. See *tenants: students*

studio *89*

style *123*

survey *50, 196*

    Royal Institute of Chartered Survey-
        ors *67*

T

taxation *31, 201*

tenancy

    assured shorthold tenancy *170*

    contractual tenancy *172*

    statutory periodic tenancy *172, 173*

    tenancy agreement *169*

    tenancy length *173*

tenants

    first-timers *76*

    'happy tenant' *27, 82, 96*

    joint tenants *32*

    long-termers *79*

    'Mr Blue-Chip' *74, 83, 179, 207*

    perfect tenant *79*

    quality applicants *22*

    rogue tenants *37*

    sharers *80, 91*

    sitting tenants *65*

    students *80*

    'tenant from hell' *84*

    tenant-like manner *138*

    tenant profiles *75*

    tenants in common *32*

    troublesome tenants *38*

    week-dayers *78*

tenure *53–64*

terraced properties *97*

tidiness *90*

tiling *112*

towel rail *120*

transport *104*

trespass *39*

trust *160*

TV *129, 157*

U

unfurnished properties *108*

upstairs *97*

utilities *51, 90, 108, 159, 169*

V

vacating a property *38*

ventilation *143*

viewings *90*

vinyl *112*

visits *37, 155–164, 159, 191*

voids *35, 74, 89, 96, 182, 208*

W

wallpaper *111*

Warren v Keen *138*

washing machines *126*

water *62, 137, 138, 159, 195, 200*

  water damage *38*

  water vapour *141*

wear and tear *37*

white goods *123, 138, 157*

White Paper *198*

windows *133, 143*

worktops *125*

Y

yield *71–72, 92*

Z

Zoopla *65*